THOMAS A HEINZ

FRANK LLOYD WRIGHT

FIELD GUIDE

METROCHICAGO   VOL 2

A. ACADEMY EDITIONS

First published in Great Britain in 1997 by
ACADEMY EDITIONS
a division of
John Wiley & Sons,
Baffins Lane, Chichester,
West Sussex PO19 1UD

ISBN: 0-471-97692-X

Other Wiley editorial offices:
New York • Weinheim • Brisbane • Singapore • Toronto

Distributed to the trade in the USA by
NATIONAL BOOK NETWORK, INC
4720 Boston Way, Lanham, Maryland 20706

Printed and bound in Singapore

CONTENTS

CONTENTS

■ There are buildings designed by Frank Lloyd Wright in thirty-five states. They number over four hundred if one includes bridges, windmills, gates and fountains. The Field Guides divide these buildings into groups of roughly equal area between the following areas: Upper Great Lakes, MetroChicago, West and East. The last two include areas outside the continental USA, such as Japan in the West volume and England in the East volume. Like most architects, Wright's first projects were for members of his family and close to home in Spring Green, and later in Oak Park. However, as his reputation grew,

he was commissioned to design buildings more far afield until he had a national practice. Overall the distribution of Wright's work follows the concentration of the population. Most of the clients were independent thinkers who were willing to put up with some of the difficulties often associated with the construction of Wright-designed buildings, such as contractors who were reluctant to tackle unusual work and bankers who were hesitant to embrace progressive ideas. In return, the clients received buildings that would give them pleasure as long as they lived.

■   This Field Guide to Wright's buildings in and around Chicago is arranged geographically, beginning to the north and ending in the southeast of the city. This organizational principle is extended to each cluster of sites and buildings.

At the back of the guide a geographical list of works gives all buildings within Illinois and Indiana alphabetically by town or city. A complete list of all of Wright's buildings is also included. It is arranged alphabetically by the last name of the original client or, if it is a commercial structure, by the proper name of the building. When a building has an alternative, popular name this is also included. Buildings featured in this and the UGL volume are identified by page number. Buildings featured in other guides in the series are identified by volume.

The primary source for the maps is the United States Geological Survey, which issues detailed topographic maps for the entire United States.

Star Ratings

The rating system used throughout the book is based on the author's opinion and takes into account several important factors: the extent to which Wright's design philosophy is expressed in the individual building; the current condition; the impact of later additions; and the ease with which the building can be viewed.

Opus Numbers

The Director of Archives at The Frank Lloyd Wright Foundation, Bruce Brooks Pfeiffer, has put together a list of all of Wright's buildings and projects and assigned a reference number to each, based on the year of the project and the chronology of projects within that year. While a few inaccuracies may appear, this has proved the best method of identifying individual designs.

GPS and UTM Numbers

The Global Positioning System (GPS) has now been accepted as an accurate locational device used in sea and air travel. A series of time-keeping satellites send their time out to a receiver which calculates the difference in times between at least three of them, giving a specific location and elevation. These GPS readings are accurate within a very narrow range. Autos and soon cellular telephones and portable computers will be fitted with these devices. GPS coordinates are included in this Field Guide as an aid to identifying locations. Like the GPS figures, the Universal Transversal Mercator (UTM) numbers are provided as an additional orientational aid.

C Numbers

These note the date that the photographs were taken by the author. C stands for circa.

AS Initials

Where (AS) appears in the text, it is a reference to Alice Sinkevitch's indispensible *AIA Guide to Chicago*, Harcourt, Brace & Co (San Diego, New York and London), 1993.

Note to Readers

The publisher and author wish to reassert to the readers that the majority of these properties are privately owned and that the owners' legal rights should be respected accordingly. The publisher and author will accept no responsibility for any action taken against any readers who contravene this notice.

Places are not merely physical things but emotional presences, resonant with the meanings each of us brings to them. Yet powerfully formed places can in themselves confer meaning and shape experience.

■ Paul Goldberger wrote this in a recent *New York Times* book review. This is for the most part why I chose to follow architecture. I could see the changes in behavior that were largely a result of building's form, color and light.

An old saying ,'the ear is the instrument of instruction and the eye is the instrument of temptation' explains why many feel that music is a higher art than painting. Architecture falls into the second category since it is experienced with the eye. Viewing architecture, however, also incorporates touch and sound. It is the art form with the greatest potential for having an effect on everyone. Wright said that 'Architecture is the Mother of all Arts.'

The sensory qualities of Wright's architecture are rarely adequately acknowledged. They are, however, evident in experiencing his buildings. Many of the ceilings in the dining rooms, for instance, are lower than other rooms. This allows for the sound to be reflected to the ceiling back to the listener in less time and with less volume, making them a space where speech is softly spoken. The colors and textures are also another interesting area of study. The earth tones, which he frequently used, have been found to have a quieting effect by those inhabiting his buildings.

Many of the Wright's best designs have now gone. They were demolished mostly through neglect and ignorance rather than for economic reasons – land was more valuable with other buildings on it. In MetroChicago, Midway Gardens, the Husser House, the Steffens House and the Fine Arts Building interiors have all been destroyed.

With all of the books that have been published on Wright and his work, it is surprising that there remain such large gaps in the information on him and his œuvre. There are many clients of whom little, if anything, is known. Buildings have been rediscovered even within the past year. Our understanding of Wright's construction methods remains partial. Many of the clients and their families have vanished. They should be located and their stories told. The stories revealed can be very compelling. The events that lead to building, and in many cases to not building the designs are more varied than anyone could imagine. The Husser family would be the perfect subject of additional inquiry. They built the largest and most elaborate pre-Prairie house. We have four photographs of the house, but little information about Husser or the Husser family. The interior photos appear to be more accidental than thoughtful. It is very important to see these lost interiors in photographs. Knowing how the Husser House was furnished and what other Wright-designed pieces might exist could greatly increase our appreciation. There are no photographs of the interiors of most of the buildings executed in the first twenty years of Wright's career. These include the Blossom, McArthur, Heller, Williams, Henderson, Hickox, Thomas, William Martin, Barton, and Cheney Houses. The fact that there exists only one known photo of Wright's uncle Jenkin Lloyd Jones's All Souls' Church is amazing since the church had a photography club from at least 1885 and there were many family activities at the church such as weddings and christenings, yet no photographs. There are also no known wedding photos of Wright's first marriage ceremony even though it was performed by Jenkin Lloyd Jones.

■ Frank Lloyd Wright lived during a time of great technological advances. He was born, in 1867, just two years after the close of the bloody Civil War and died in 1959, just two years after the Russians launched the first satellite, Sputnik. He saw the beginnings of the automobile and the airplane, electricity and indoor plumbing. His buildings reflect this without it becoming obvious or overpowering. Many of his technological building advances are still not permitted by building officials today; although they were much more ahead of their, and our, time than they are unsafe by any standards.

The area of MetroChicago encompasses seven counties in two states. The area contains the largest concentration of Wright buildings anywhere. The Prairie buildings appeal to many today perhaps because they are closer in many ways to the buildings that we live in now. The later Usonian designs are more advanced than the typical American home and tend to stand in less formal surroundings, rural some might say.

For Wright, Chicago represented the architectural 'Promised Land', the land of milk and honey. As well as a boom town – the population doubled in every decade between 1840 and 1910 – it was a progressive urban center where many new ideas were tested in architecture by new thinking on the part of the clients as well as the architects. There were engineers and builders eager to lend their hand. Chicago is the location for nearly one quarter of Wright's existing buildings. Many family members, neighbors and business associates put thier faith in his work and supported, enthusiastically, his ideas. The city was large enough to make him seem less outlandish than he might have appeared in a smaller city with fewer architects.

Wright wrote to his uncle Jenkin Lloyd Jones, in August of 1885, concerning the design of the Helena Valley Chapel at Spring Green, before Jones hired Joseph Lyman Silsbee as the architect. Wright said that he had already completed some sketches for the design and was ready to alter it to meet his uncle's wishes. Given Wright's aggressive personality even at this early date, it is possible that he was involved from the start and had contact with Silsbee during the entire design and construction phases. Wright appears not to have attended the second term at the University of Wisconsin in 1886 and instead may have gone to Chicago and worked for Silsbee in the middle of the year. He said that he saw Silsbee's second design for Jones, All Souls' Church in Chicago, under construction. The church, which was situated on the southeast corner of Langley and Oakwood (40th Street), was built between March and August 1886.

In *An Autobiography*, Wright states that he first came to Chicago in the spring of 1887 and stumbled upon a certain theatrical production of *Sieba*. Contrary to his statements, however, this was performed at Adler & Sullivan's Chicago Opera House in late August 1886, not during the spring of 1887. Wright was most likely in Chicago during the summer of 1886 rather than that of the next year.

Wright may have been persuaded to return for the third term at the University of Wisconsin in September 1886, but may have decided to return to Chicago later in the year. He was employed by Mr Clay, later of Beers, Clay & Dutton, in a position that was over his head in early 1887, or at least until April or May, when the information for the Chicago directory was compiled. Realizing Clay's work was more than he could handle, he appealed to Silsbee who took him back. The directories do not show Wright employed at Silsbee's office at any time, but at Clay's, Room 88 at 175 Dearborn.

The 1887 directory listed Wright as an architect not a draftsman. Wright lived in his uncle's neighborhood at John A Waterman's house, 3921 South Vincennes. Waterman's son, Harry, was a draftsman in Silsbee's office. The Vincennes home was west and then north and around the corner from All Souls' Church. With a neighborhood resident and his nephew both working at Silsbee's, this might explain why there are no letters to or from Silsbee in the letter files of Jenkin Lloyd Jones concerning the design or construction of the Spring Green Chapel or the Chicago Church.

After a second stint in Silsbee's office in the late spring of 1887, Wright must have decided he needed to improve his position and was hired at Adler & Sullivan at a fantastic rate of $25.00 per week or $1,250 per year. Wright said his employment at Adler & Sullivan was to begin just before Sullivan was to leave for an architect's convention in St Louis. This convention occurred in November 1887. It was also in November that Wright's first building for his aunt's Hillside Home School, just west of the Unity Chapel of Silsbee's design, opened its doors.

Two drawings by Wright were published in March and May 1888 in *Inland Architect*. They were for the JL Cochran and the William Waller Houses, both designed by Silsbee. In June, Wright's rendering of the Victor Falkeneau Houses designed by Adler & Sullivan was published in the same magazine.

On Wright's twenty-first birthday, 8 June 1888, he exercised his new right to own land by purchasing a corner lot at Chicago and Forest in Oak Park. He bought the land from EO Gale, the father of two of his early clients, Thomas and Walter Gale. The property is located across the street to the west of where Wright would build his own house one year later. The source of funds for this purchase is unknown but it may have come from his mother, Anna, who had sold the library of her late husband William Wright, and had a 'little money' from the sale of her father's farm. The property was purchased just after Anna Wright had moved to Oak Park from Madison, Wisconsin. Anna was living at 214 Forest Avenue with Frank and his sister Maginel in the house of Unitarian minister Augusta Chapin. Frank's land was sold just after the purchase of the property across the street at 428 Forest. It appears that Wright made a profit on the transaction selling it back to EO Gale for $3,950 on 17 June 1889.

The year 1889 was one of many busy years in Wright's life. He bought the east corner lot at Forest and Chicago Avenues for $2,875 on 5 May 1889 from John and Jane Blair who had moved to British Columbia, Canada. Wright married Catherine Tobin on 1 June 1889. The ceremony was performed by Wright's uncle, Jenkin Lloyd Jones.

Wright was working at Adler & Sullivan's offices in a building of their own design, the Borden Block. In early 1889 they moved to a new office in the tallest building in Chicago, The Auditorium Tower. In 1890, a plan of the Adler & Sullivan offices was published showing four private offices, one each for Adler, Sullivan and Paul Mueller. The office featured a glass partition separating Wright from the rest of the drafting room and had a door with direct access to Sullivan's office. The famous contract that Wright signed in order to acquire the $5,000 to build his house was with Louis Sullivan personally, and not with the firm. The 19 August 1889 contract contained no provisions pertaining to outside work, sometimes termed 'moonlighting.' In fact, it was to Sullivan's advantage to allow Wright to work outside the office insuring that he would be repaid. The terms are enlightening. The interest was at 6 per cent per annum due on the outstanding balance and payable monthly. The principal was to be paid monthly at $500 for the first year, $750 for both the second and third years, $1,000 for the fourth and the balance, $2,000, the fifth year. This would indicate that Wright was to receive raises, perhaps in proportion to the increases of the loan repayment. With his starting salary of only $25 per week or $100 per month, the loan would put Wright in a difficult financial position. Rough calculations suggest that principal and interest would come to a total of $64 per month for the first year leaving about $40 or $10 per week for living expenses. Payment would increase to $81 for the second and third years, to $98 for the fourth and to $176 per month for the fifth year. There are no records that track Wright's income or which show that any of the payments were made. About the time Wright may have left Adler & Sullivan's employment, in the late summer of 1893, Wright repaid Sullivan $5,775. From the total, it appears that few of the scheduled payments had been made.

On 21 August 1889, Anna Lloyd Wright purchased the lot just east of her son's from the same Blairs who had sold Wright the west half of the lot. The property included a small Gothic house that may have been built by the Blairs, perhaps as early as 1866, after they had bought the property from Henry Austin. In the 1890 *Chicago City Directory*, Wright is listed as working at 1600 Auditorium Tower and residing in Oak Park.

Wright may have left Sullivan's office for several reasons. There was a depression that began in the spring of 1893 and deepened as the summer wore on. A note published about the condition of Adler & Sullivan indicated that there were only three employees left by August. Outside the firm, Wright had won a competition for two boathouses in Madison, Wisconsin. He also entered the Milwaukee Library competition with a classical design that reminded many of the façade of the Louvre in Paris.

William Winslow, who Wright often referred to as the first of his clients in independent architectural practice, did not purchase his property until November 1894. The commission was announced as early as June in a local publication. The Clark House in La Grange was completed, photographed and published. Wright and Cecil Corwin shared office space in Room 1501 in Adler & Sullivan's Schiller Building.

A piece of land near the northwest corner of Harlem and Lake Street was to prove a very fertile one for Wright. First, in 1898, the River Forest Golf Club was located here – a small nine-hole course – which was replaced by the River Forest Tennis Club. This building was later moved west several blocks and expanded. The southeast corner of the block was also occupied by the Cummings's Real Estate Office for several years.

There have been several discussions about Wright being ostracized after his return from his 1909–11 sojourn with Mamah Cheney. These personal events did not have as great an impact on Wright's ability to attract paying clients as was previously thought. His post-Europe projects that were designed and built were many in number. These included the Booth House, Midway Gardens, the San Francisco Call Building, the American Systems House and others. He also planned on having a small office on the near north side of Chicago's Loop on Goethe Street while most of the drafting would occur at his home and main studio, Taliesin.

Midway Gardens, designed for the Wallers on the southwest corner of 60th and Cottage Grove, was a great step forward in the integration of architecture, sculpture, graphics and music. It is such a shame that Midway Gardens was so short lived and its spatial complexities so little appreciated or commented upon at the time.

Albert M Johnson commissioned Wright in 1924 to design a new building for the National Life Insurance Co, proposed for a site on Michigan Avenue at Chicago Avenue, on the north side of Water Tower Square. It was to be a copper and glass tower. If it had been built, this building could have changed the direction of Wright's professional career and put him at the forefront of the designers of tall buildings. It most certainly would have become a Chicago landmark. Johnson's own house still stands at Sheridan Road and Devon Avenue on the lake.

Wright's last constructed Oak Park design was the 1913 Harry Adams House and his last built Chicago design was the 1916 Emil Bach House. There was a scattering of Usonian houses in the 1930s, 40s and 50s in the distant suburbs including two Erdman Prefabs. His most spectacular MetroChicago design was the Illinois Mile High. This skyscraper continues to capture the imagination of many, indeed it was recently announced that an elevator has been developed that would make the Mile High a viable project. Several other manufacturers, suppliers and engineers have made similar statements over the years revealing their fascination with the concept.

Frank Lloyd Wright remains the source of inspiration to many architects, clients and material suppliers. His position carries on growing beyond any reasonable expectations, as his work continues extending its meaning.

Bedroom wing of the Avery Coonley House, Riverside, Ill, c1911

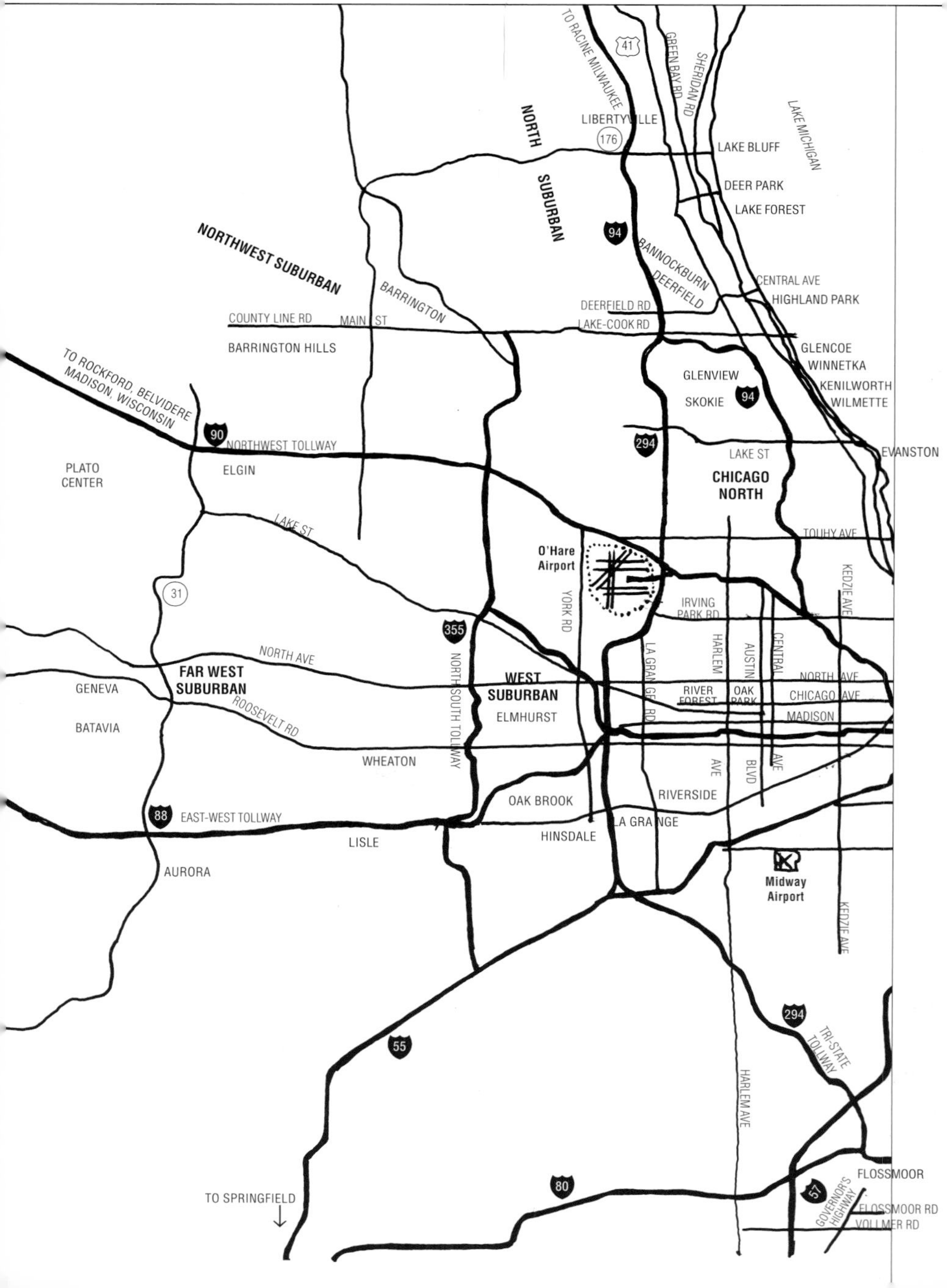
TO RACINE MILWAUKEE
41
GREEN BAY RD
SHERIDAN RD
LAKE MICHIGAN
NORTH SUBURBAN
LIBERTYVILLE
176
LAKE BLUFF
DEER PARK
LAKE FOREST
94
BANNOCKBURN
DEERFIELD
NORTHWEST SUBURBAN
BARRINGTON
CENTRAL AVE
HIGHLAND PARK
DEERFIELD RD
COUNTY LINE RD
MAIN ST
LAKE-COOK RD
BARRINGTON HILLS
GLENCOE
WINNETKA
GLENVIEW
KENILWORTH
SKOKIE
WILMETTE
TO ROCKFORD, BELVIDERE
MADISON, WISCONSIN
90
NORTHWEST TOLLWAY
294
EVANSTON
LAKE ST
PLATO CENTER
ELGIN
CHICAGO NORTH
LAKE ST
TOUHY AVE
O'Hare Airport
KEDZIE AVE
31
YORK RD
IRVING PARK RD
355
LA GRANGE RD
HARLEM
AUSTIN
CENTRAL
NORTH AVE
FAR WEST SUBURBAN
WEST SUBURBAN
NORTH AVE
GENEVA
RIVER FOREST
OAK PARK
CHICAGO AVE
ROOSEVELT RD
NORTH-SOUTH TOLLWAY
ELMHURST
MADISON
BATAVIA
WHEATON
AVE
BLVD
AVE
OAK BROOK
RIVERSIDE
88
EAST-WEST TOLLWAY
LA GRANGE
HINSDALE
LISLE
Midway Airport
AURORA
KEDZIE AVE
294
TRI-STATE TOLLWAY
55
HARLEM AVE
FLOSSMOOR
80
57
GOVERNOR'S HIGHWAY
TO SPRINGFIELD
FLOSSMOOR RD
VOLLMER RD

■ This area contains the largest concentration of Wright designs, encompassing the earliest existing building of his career, his 1889 Oak Park home, as well as the 1959 Allan Friedman House at Bannockburn. It has a full complement of his work. The great majority date from his most formative years, 1889 to 1916, a period in which fewer records were kept, such as building permits. Time works against records. This additional twenty years inserts an extra generation that often might have considered the papers of their elders of little worth, discarding letters, photographs and other materials. It is most unfortunate that this has happened but too late to reverse.

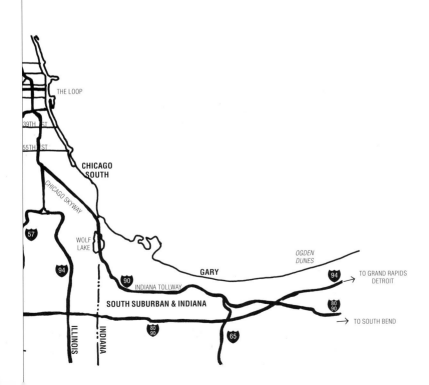

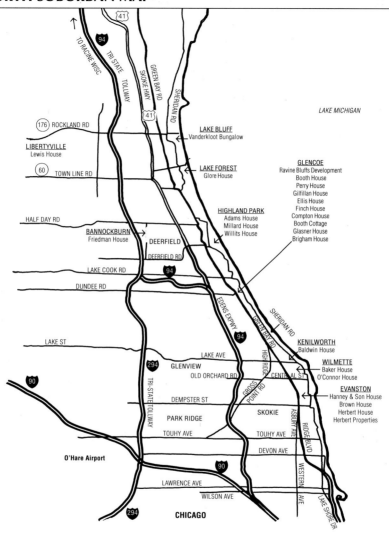

To Racine Wisc.
Tri State Tollway
94
41
Green Bay Rd
Skokie Hwy
Sheridan Rd
LAKE MICHIGAN

176 ROCKLAND RD
LAKE BLUFF
Vanderkloot Bungalow

LIBERTYVILLE
Lewis House

60 TOWN LINE RD
LAKE FOREST
Glore House

GLENCOE
Ravine Bluffs Development
Booth House
Perry House
Gilfillan House
Ellis House
Finch House
Compton House
Booth Cottage
Glasner House
Brigham House

HIGHLAND PARK
Adams House
Millard House
Willits House

HALF DAY RD

BANNOCKBURN
Friedman House
DEERFIELD
DEERFIELD RD

LAKE COOK RD
94
DUNDEE RD

Edens Expwy
Green Bay Rd
Sheridan Rd

LAKE ST
94

KENILWORTH
Baldwin House

LAKE AVE
294 **GLENVIEW**
OLD ORCHARD RD
CENTRAL ST
High Ridge

WILMETTE
Baker House
O'Connor House

EVANSTON
Hanney & Son House
Brown House
Herbert House
Herbert Properties

DEMPSTER ST
SKOKIE
Gross Point Rd
Asbury Ave
Ridge Blvd

90
TRI-STATE TOLLWAY

PARK RIDGE
TOUHY AVE
TOUHY AVE
DEVON AVE

O'Hare Airport
90
Western Ave
Lake Shore Dr

LAWRENCE AVE
WILSON AVE
294 **CHICAGO**

■ The northern suburbs have the wealthiest population in the region. The cool breezes of Lake Michigan temper the hot summers here and the water keeps the winters a few degrees warmer than the hinterlands to the west. A good commuter rail service and then the Chicago Fire of 1871 helped to provide the incentive to move out of the city and develop these small villages. It was not just the wealthy who made the trek but people of all classes. Green Bay Road was a former Native American trail.

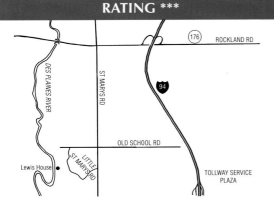

LLOYD LEWIS HOUSE
153 Little St Mary's Road
Libertyville, Illinois 60048
1940 4008

GPS:	N 42 15.452
	W 87 55.871
UTM:	16 T 042 3193
	467 8790

Directions: West of Interstate 94 between Townline and Rockland is St Mary's Road. Little St Mary's Road goes west of St Mary's 1.2 miles north of Townline. Go west on Little St Mary's to the house number.

Accessibility: The house cannot be seen from the road or approached without encroaching on the residents' privacy.

■ Born in 1891, Lewis moved to Chicago from Philadelphia in 1915. He was the drama critic and editor of the *Chicago Daily News*. Though he gave his main hobby as farming, he lived near Sherman Park on 54th Street in Chicago before moving to Libertyville.

    The house is a few feet from the Des Plaines River which occasionally floods. For this reason, the house is raised above grade. Though the materials are typical of Wright's Usonian designs, the raised main rooms make it unique. The porch off the living room was originally open, it was only later that he designed the screened enclosure.   c76

WILLIAM J VANDERKLOOT BUNGALOW
(American Systems Bungalow)
231 Prospect Avenue
Lake Bluff, Illinois 60044
1916 1506

GPS: N 42 16.702
      W 87 50.443
UTM: 16 T 043 0678

Directions: Exit Interstate 94 or Route 41 at Highway 176, proceed east for 1.7 miles on Center Avenue to Evanston Avenue, then proceed south one block to Prospect Avenue and east on Prospect to the address, about a half block.

Accessibility: The house can be seen from the street, through some foliage.

■ This house has never been thoroughly researched. I only discovered it in 1975 when I was driving around looking for a possible Adler & Sullivan house which had been demolished before it could be documented. It is very close in style to the O'Connor House of Wilmette (p37) and it also has simple art glass. The house was built after May 1917 for summer rental by William J Vanderkloot who lived across the street and owned several other properties in the neighborhood. It was sold to two sisters, Ida and Grace McElwain, who also rented it out during the summer season. c74

(The demolished Angster House, Opus # 1101, was built in 1911 and located on the north side of town at the lake on Blodget Road near the ravine, see map.)

HERBERT F GLORE HOUSE
170 North Mayflower
Lake Forest, Illinois 60045
1951 5107

GPS: N 42 14.572
W 87 49.190
UTM: 16 T 043 2362
467 7067

Directions: The streets of Lake Forest curve around. Be careful to follow the map. Exit Route 41 east on Deerpath past Green Bay Road (1 mile from 41) and through downtown Lake Forest, over the railroad tracks to Mayflower (2 miles from 41). Drive south on Mayflower (0.8 miles) to the address. The house is on the west side of the street.

Accessibility: The house can be seen from the street.

■ The Glore House is different from other 1950s houses. It is small with a large gable roof and is one of the few houses that has a full two-story living room. The bedrooms are on the second floor. Jack Howe drafted the drawings for the house and repeated many of the same elements in his own work after Wright's death in 1959. The house has had many owners and suffered as a result of this.   c73

   (The Harold McCormick House was designed in 1907 for a site east of the Glore House, at the bluff along the shore of Lake Michigan. Mrs Angster, see p18, is believed to have been the private secretarty of McCormick's wife.)

ALLAN FRIEDMAN HOUSE
200 Thornapple Road
Bannockburn, Illinois 60015
1959 5624

GPS: 42 11.651
      87 52.304

Directions: Bannockburn is between Interstate 94 and Route 41. Go south of Half Day Road on Telegraph to Hilltop for a block then proceed south on Thornapple Road to the address. The house is on the west side of Thornapple. The house is north of Deerfield Road. East of Route 41 Deerfield Road becomes Central Avenue in Highland Park.

Accessibility: Only brick walls can be seen from the private street.

■ This is probably the last house that was constructed while Wright was alive. It is on a large but rather flat 5-acre site. The Friedmans received their plans in 1956 but started construction much later. The house has no particular artistic flourish. Overall, it is a quiet design of red brick with Philippine mahogany detailing. The large brick mass that extends above the roof includes a kitchen skylight. Such skylights occur frequently in Wright's Usonian houses. The increased height of the kitchen ceiling allows for the ventilation of heat and cooking odors. The Friedmans thought about enclosing the carport as a garage but hesitated, not wanting to obscure Wright's design. c72

MARY MW ADAMS HOUSE
1923 Lake Avenue
Highland Park, Illinois 60035
1905 0501

GPS: N 42 11.251
W 87 47.320

Directions: Exit Interstate 94 at Deerfield Road eastbound. Deerfield becomes Central Avenue at Route 41. Drive east into Highland Park. Continue on Central to Lake Avenue, 1.7 miles from 41, and turn south one block. The Adams House is on the southeast corner of Lake and Laurel.

Accessibility: All sides of the house can be seen from public property.

■ Mary Adams lived here for a very short time, probably less than three years. She was perhaps Wright's oldest client. She was seventy when she commissioned him. She died a few years after the house was completed and her ashes were sent to Hot Springs, Arkansas, presumably to members of her family. There are very few public documents which tell us about her long life, except that she was very involved in the Christian Science Church. Nothing is known about her family or how she came to engage Wright as the designer of the house.   c96

(The Alfred Ellinwood House was designed for a site nearby Highland Park, in Deerfield, but no location can be determined and nothing else is known about it. Opus# 4102.)

GEORGE MADISON MILLARD HOUSE
1689 Lake Avenue
Highland Park, Illinois 60035
1906 0606

GPS: N 42 11.251
W 87 47.138
UTM: 16 T 043 5127
467 0895

Directions: The Millard House is three blocks, 0.4 miles, south of the Adams House on Lake Avenue. It is on the east side of the street.

Accessibility: The house is visible from the street in winter.

■ Millard worked for AC McClurg's bookstore on Wabash, in downtown Chicago, from 1866 until about 1908 when he moved to South Pasadena with his wife. He started the 'Saints & Sinners' corner at the store. This was the site of many debates and presentations by prominent literary figures, including the famous author Eugene Field who wrote about Millard's 'bookmanship.' As the dealer in fine and rare books, he knew Williams (see p54), as well as many of Wright's other clients, including Browne (see p134). Millard was born in 1846 and in 1901, at fifty-five, married Alice Parsons, a twenty-eight-year-old Chicago school teacher, in London. Alice had another house, La Miniatura, designed for her by Wright in Pasadena (West volume). c96

(Across the street to the south is a WW Boynton-designed log cabin for an unrelated family of Millards, who donated the property to Millard Park.)

WARD W WILLITS HOUSE
1445 Sheridan Road
Highland Park, Illinois 60035
1901 0208

GPS: N 42 10.757
W 87 47.232
UTM: 16 T 043 4989
466 9982

Directions: For some reason north–south Sheridan Road is not continuous as it runs through downtown Highland Park. Exit Interstate 94 at Deerfield Road to the east. Continue about 3 miles and pass over Highway 41, (or exit 41 eastbound) for 1.1 miles; from 41, the street name changes to Central Avenue. Continue into town and cross the railroad tracks to St John's Avenue. Turn south on St John's for two long blocks, 0.3 miles, to south Sheridan Road. Take Sheridan Road to the east and continue for 0.5 miles. The house is on the east side of the street at Waverly.

Accessibility: Do not venture onto the property, the front of the house can be seen from the street. Wright's famous perspective of the house was taken from a viewpoint at the intersection of the driveway and the sidewalk. This angle is also the best for taking photographs of the house.   c93

■ This is the first great house of Wright's Prairie period. Willits was born in 1859 at New Boston, Illinois, on the Mississippi River. He worked for Adams & Westlake Brass & Bronze Foundry and may have known William Winslow through business (see p52).

Willits became chairman of the board of the company and died at ninety-two. Adams & Westlake employed Orlando Giannini, Wright's main art-glass supplier, for some years. Despite this connection, it is not known if Willits and Giannini knew each other at this or any other time. Willits and his wife went with Wright and his wife, Catherine, to Japan in 1905. When Wright and Wes Peters stopped by the house in the late 1940s, Mrs Willits opened the door and greeted them as if they had just been by weeks before. Wright had supposedly not spoken to Willits since they fell out sometime before 1910. Willits lived in the house until his death in 1952.

Several rare photographs of the construction of the Willits House survive. These show typical balloon framing in the walls. The wall studs in balloon framing extend from the foundation continuously to the roof without a break for the second floor. In these photos there is no evidence of the steel frame that now exists. There is a small truss in the attic space that is supported by the steel columns in the walls. This truss in turn has steel rods extending through the inside corners of the second-floor corner balconies that help to support the living-room ceiling. These steel members do not appear in these photographs.

Just above the base on both sides of the living room are what at first appear to be windows. In fact, these are cold air ducts for the heating system that runs along the long walls of the room. There are ducts in the basement that contain several large pipes which release heat into two thin grilles located just inside the built-in oak bookcases.

The house has been sensitively restored and relandscaped by its current owners.

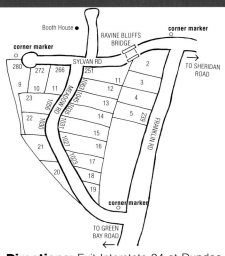

RAVINE BLUFFS DEVELOPMENT
Meadow and Sylvan Roads
Glencoe, Illinois 60022
1915 1516

GPS: N 42 08.606
W 87 45.834
UTM: 16 T 043 6878
466 5984

Directions: Exit Interstate 94 at Dundee eastbound to the dead end at Green Bay Road (see map on p33). Turn north about two blocks, then turn east over the railroad tracks and keep to the left or north. The first corner marker is on the northwest corner of Franklin and Maple Hill about one hundred feet north of Maple Hill on Franklin. The second marker is further north on Franklin at Sylvan Road and the third is west to the cul-de-sac at the west end of Sylvan Road. These three markers roughly define the extent of the development. All of the Booth related buildings are within these boundaries.

■ The original scheme would have transformed this part of Glencoe with its Wright-designed railroad stations and town hall. Only the planning of the scheme was fully realized. The client agreed with Wright on what was to be built, but the execution was incomplete. The buildings that were built were constructed several years later.

In July 1911, Elizabeth K Booth was listed as the new owner of a large piece of property, purchased from Sylvan Newhall. The land was re-subdivided in August 1914.

Booth was the client of all of the Wright designs in this development. There were at least seven designed for these lots that can be identified. There may have been as many as twenty-five. The public records in city directories and county property documents name subsequent tenants and owners. Other authors have associated the buildings with second, third and fourth owners. Curiously, there are building permits for only four of the five Wright-designed rental houses. These are all dated 28 October 1915.

The bridge was approved by the Glencoe City Council on 30 March 1915, according to research undertaken by Susan Solway with Susan Benjamin (*Ravine Bluffs Bridge*, United States Department of the Interior, HAER, No IL-14). Susan Solway has also discovered that a Wright-designed railroad shelter was constructed in about 1911, which survived until the 1950s (see Carla Lind, *Lost Wright*, 1996).

(The Elizabeth Stone House design of 1906 has been published, but little is known about the client. I believe she was the daughter of Melville Stone, the founder of the *Chicago Daily News* and sister of publisher Herbert Stone of Stone & Kimball. In 1906, she bought a 5-acre lot from her father east of Sheridan and Booth's land.)

SHERMAN BOOTH HOUSE
265 Sylvan Road
Glencoe, Illinois 60022
1915 1502

Directions: Once at the development, locate the corner of Franklin and Sylvan. Proceed west on Sylvan one block to Meadow and turn north. The Booth House is on the west side of the street.

Accessibility: The house is set back from the street from where it is only partially visible.

■ Booth was Wright's attorney and the brother of Mrs Angster (see p18). The first design for Booth's house is one of Wright's most beautiful renderings. The house was to be entered via a bridge spanning the ravine. The actual building is a remodeling of two earlier structures, one being the stable, and is the realization of Wright's second design for Booth. Some of Wright's best designs for furniture were executed for this house, but only the canopy beds and the floor lamps remain in place. A dining-room set was built but only a few chairs have been located.

Booth is first listed at this address in a 1917 city directory. The building permit, number 333, for this house was dated 14 April 1916. The design program was for a residence 108 feet wide by 50 feet deep and 34 feet high. It was to cost $16,000, which was good value at the time. This structure combines a garage and stable that intersect at the new, taller part of the building. At one time there was a U-shaped driveway that extended from Sylvan to the house, making a much more elegant entry. c75

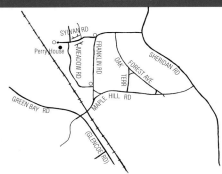

LOT 10: CHARLES R PERRY HOUSE
Ravine Bluffs Housing
272 Sylvan Roads
Glencoe, Illinois 60022
1915 1516

GPS: N 42 08.606
W 87 45.834

Directions: Meadow and Franklin are parallel to each other and perpendicular to Sylvan. The house is at the west end of Sylvan at the third boundary mark.

Accessibility: Evergreen trees obscure views of the house. Only small portions of the house can be seen.

■ According to Cook County records, the editor Charles R Perry bought this property in 1918 from Elizabeth Booth. Perry is first recorded as living here in the 1920-21 city directory. He is the first resident noted at this address. In 1922 Perry bought Lot 11 to the east from Booth, reselling it later. Wright also made a design for the corner lot. The house at the corner of Sylvan and Meadow was built in 1996.

Perry was cited in the city directory as the Secretary of the Rotary Club. His wife was Jessie B Perry. There are no further records of Perry in Chicago or the surrounding suburbs that might help locate the family. c74

LOT 22: SJ GILFILLAN HOUSE
Ravine Bluffs Housing
1030 Meadow Road
Glencoe, Illinois 60022
1915 1516

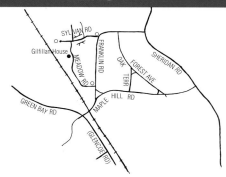

Directions: This house is on the west side of Meadow south of Sylvan.

Accessibility: The main façade can be seen from the street.

■ There are four lots on the west side of Meadow but only one has a house built upon it. Booth sold Lot 22 to Hollis Reed Root in 1921 and Lot 23, to the north, and Lot 21, to the south, in 1922. The city directory listed SJ Gilfillan at this address in 1920 and 1921. Root was noted as being in advertising as were most of these second owners. He is listed in the 1922-23 volume with his wife Helen J Root. There is no mention of the particular companies that the neighbors worked for.

We know from a second building permit (#282) issued for the house, dated 28 October 1915, some eight years after it was built, that the garage was an addition. A drawing of the original design shows an open south porch. Drawings for this building were published in Brian Spencer's *Prairie School Tradition*. This house has the same floor plan as that of Lot 10 to the north.   c74

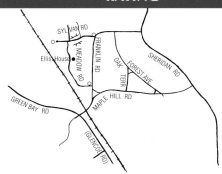

LOT 15: CJ ELLIS HOUSE
Ravine Bluffs Housing
1031 Meadow Road
Glencoe, Illinois 60022
1916 1605

Directions: The house is across the street to the east from Lot 22. It is the furthest north of the three Wright designs on the east side of the street.

Accessibility: Three sides of the house can be seen.

■ In May of 1918 Herbert Angster bought this lot from Booth, presumably with a house on it. This is the most unique of all the five rental houses. William E and Eva L Kier bought the property from Angster in 1919 but the city directory, published the following year, listed CJ Ellis, jr, as residing here. The 1922 edition of *Polk's Directory* shows the Roots and their daughters, Elenora and Vivian, at this address. Kier is also noted as being in advertising.

Like other owners of houses in Ravine Bluffs, there is no other information about the Kiers. It would be nice if the descendants would come forward and let us know about their family.   c74

LOT 16: FRANK B FINCH HOUSE
Ravine Bluffs Housing
1027 Meadow Road
Glencoe, Illinois 60022
1915 1516

Directions: This house is between the two other Wright designs on the east side of Meadow .

Accessibility: Like other houses in this area, it can be seen from the street.

■ In 1916 Frank B Finch was listed as residing at 240 Meadow and was the only resident on Meadow in the directory, but only for this single year. The county records show that Finch bought the property from Sherman Booth in July 1916. There is no building permit for this lot as there are for the other four houses. Wright's drawings are dated 15 October 1915, and are signed and dated by Finch 20 November 1915. Sherman bought back the property in May 1920 and sold it to William W and Dorothy Ross in July 1921. There is no listing for anyone at this address or under any of the names associated with the house in the 1920-21 directory. Ross, also in advertising, appears first in the 1922-23 issue. The entry addition on the northwest corner was built later as may be guessed by the pink paint on its exterior.   c74

LOT 17: JM COMPTON HOUSE
Ravine Bluffs Housing
1023 Meadow Road
Glencoe, Illinois 60022
1915 1516

Directions: This house is the southernmost Wright-designed house on the block.

Accessibility: It can be seen from the street.

■ Wright's drawings are dated 21 and 22 October 1915, just a week before they were submitted for the building permit. This is the second property that Angster bought from Sherman Booth, also in May 1918. Angster held onto it for about two years, only selling it to JM Compton in May 1920. A couple of years later, in April 1922, he sold it to Johnson, but he apparently backed out or defaulted because Compton then sold it to Daniel E and Lute F Kissam in May 1922. The 1920-21 city directory lists JM Compton at this address with his wife Dorothy. Compton was a publisher at that time. Kissam was working in cotton duck according to the 1922 directory. On the drawings Wright's office address is given as 600 Orchestra Hall (see p134). This was just below the Cliff Dwellers' Club, where Sullivan was spending much of his time at this date.   c74

SHERMAN BOOTH COTTAGE
239 Franklin Street
Glencoe, Illinois 60022
1911 1119

Directions: The cottage is in the center of the block on the west side of the street.

Accessibility: Set to the rear of the lot, the house can be seen from the street but is more visible in winter.

■ The cottage was first published in the *Frank Lloyd Wright Newsletter* in May 1978. It is a very simple one-story building that according to local custom was moved to its current site when the main house was built further west, across the ravine. There are few architectural features but the living-room windows retain the simple ladder motif art glass.

Sherman Booth had his attorney's offices in the Borland Building and lived in Chicago before moving to this building in Glencoe (see also p26). He is first noted in the 1914-15 city directory as living at 201 Franklin. This must be at the north end of this block, perhaps even north of where Sylvan crosses it. According to a building permit dated 10 February 1913, the house was 51 feet wide by 21 feet deep and nine feet high. The cost was to be $1,000. Elizabeth K Booth was listed as the owner on the building permit. By 1917, a PJ Woolf was listed at 239 Franklin.   c76

WILLIAM A GLASNER HOUSE
850 Sheridan Road
Glencoe, Illinois 60022
1905 0505

GPS:	N 42 08.480
	W 87 45.283
UTM:	16 T 043 7635
	466 5744

Directions: The Glasner House is on Sheridan Road just south of Maple Hill Road on the west side of the street behind the bridge on the south side of the ravine.

Accessibility: The front of the house can be seen from the street. There are no sidewalks on Sheridan at this point and no parking. A curve in the road is just to the south and one must be careful driving.

■ William Argall Glasner worked for the First National Bank of Chicago as did Frank Baker of Wilmette (see p36). He was married to Gora Lillian Glasner. According to Susan Solway, the design of this house came out of a competition by Glasner for a two-person dwelling without servants. Wright seems to have won. This is one of several innovative designs that incorporated an octagonal pavilion, including his own studio's library and another similar unit for the Bagley House of Hinsdale (p101). Glasner moved sometime after 1916 and there are no further records of his movements. In recent times storm windows have been installed over the art glass, degrading the appearance of the wonderful iridescent glass. c96

EDMUND F BRIGHAM HOUSE
790 Sheridan Road
Glencoe, Illinois 60022
1915 1503

GPS: N 42 08.380
     W 87 45.280
UTM: 16 T 043 7637
     466 5559

Directions: The house is the third house north of Beach on the west side of Sheridan.

Accessibility: The front of the house can be seen from the street.

■ Brigham worked for the Chicago and Northwestern Railroad as a general freight agent. He and his wife, Edith A, lived on Sheridan Road north of Beach (then Central) at the time of the 1904 city directory. According to records in the county recorder's office, Brigham bought land here first in December 1901 from Sylvan Newhall and then in January 1904 from Dora Parry. He sold off pieces of it over several years until the lot for the Wright design was all that remained. His brother Henry lived on Greenleaf on the same block to the west. There was no building permit for this house, or for the stables at the rear which were demolished in the late 1960s. The date of the design is open to question. Susan Solway believes it may be as early as 1906-08, contemporary with the Evans House (p128). When Brigham died in 1921 his widow moved to Greenleaf near her family. c74

(It is unlikely that Wright's design for Grace Fuller was ever realized, as suggested by others, as there is no evidence in the property records of her building or owning land.)

HIRAM BALDWIN HOUSE
205 South Essex
Kenilworth, Illinois 60043
1905 0502

GPS:	N 42 05.248
	W 87 42.588
UTM:	16 T 044 1296
	465 9731

Directions: Kenilworth is situated on the lake between the towns of Winnetka to the north and Wilmette to the south. Unlike most other street grids, Kenilworth's streets are not set on the compass directions. The house is on Essex two blocks south of Kenilworth Avenue. It is on the east side of the street at the north corner.

Accessibility: The house can be seen from the street.

■ The entry to the Baldwin House has been altered and the small wings on the front of the porch removed from the faceted bay to the detriment of the design. Nearly all the art glass has been extracted except for a few lights at the back of the house. These art glass designs are similar to those in the William E Martin House (p82) and are the basis for some of the patterns in the Dana House (East volume).   c80

In 1895, Wright designed an unbuilt project for Jessie Baldwin (Opus# 9508) for Oak Park. It is not known if the two Baldwins were related.

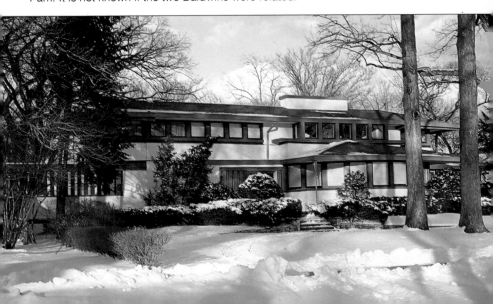

FRANK J BAKER HOUSE
507 Lake Avenue
Wilmette, Illinois 60091
1909 0901

GPS: N 42 04.711
W 87 41.678
UTM: 16 T 044 0819
465 7255

Directions: Lake Avenue runs east and west through Wilmette and crosses Sheridan Road on the east and Highway 41/Interstate 94, Edens Expressway, on the west. The Baker House is two blocks west of Sheridan on the south side of Lake Avenue. It is about 4 miles from Edens Expressway, Route 41, and 0.3 miles east of Green Bay Road.

Accessibility: The front of the house is screened by evergreen trees. One can see only glimpses of the building, making photography of the subject frustrating.

■ Baker was a vice-president of Samuel Insull's North Shore Electric Company until about 1917. He subsequently went into private law practice and became the President of the First National Bank of Chicago. While at the Electric Company he is credited with having extended electric street lighting to the suburbs. He lived in the house for about fifteen years. The house was noted as vacant in a 1925 directory.   c71

JJ O'CONNOR HOUSE
(American Systems Bungalow)
330 Gregory
Wilmette, Illinois 60091
1916 1506

GPS: N 42 04.224
W 87 41.423
UTM: 16 T 044 2887
465 7823

Directions: Central Street is a major thoroughfare in northern Evanston. It is one block north of Old Orchard Road off Edens Expressway, Interstate 94. A few blocks east of Green Bay Road and the Chicago & Northwestern Railroad viaduct is Northwestern University's Dyche Stadium. Ashland runs north–south on the west side of Dyche and intersects Central at a stoplight. Take Ashland north, crossing Isabella, one block to Gregory. Turn east for two blocks and look for the address.

Accessibility: The front of the house can be seen in all seasons.

■ This is another example of the Richards Brothers American Systems Bungalow. It is virtually identical to those built in Milwaukee (see UGL volume). The first resident was JJ O'Connor who was a real-estate broker. A Mr Burleigh, who was listed as a salesman in the 1925 city directory, occupied the house by 1922. There have been a few changes to the interior and the entry porch has been enclosed. There may be more of these houses that have not yet been documented. Please report back if you locate a candidate.   c95

HANNEY & SON HOUSE
(American Systems House)
2614 Lincolnwood
Evanston, Illinois 60201
1916 1506

GPS: N42 03.908
      W 87 42.919

Directions: The Hanney & Son House is on Lincolnwood, just north of Central, at the stoplight. Lincolnwood is halfway between Crawford and Green Bay Road.

Accessibility: The south side of the house can be seen across a parking lot from Central. The front is also visible from the street.

■ This is another example of the American Systems Ready-Cut. There are hundreds of drawings in the Taliesin Archives for this system but none of the buildings that were built were exactly like the drawings. The system obviously allowed for considerable customizing in order to suit each site and the wishes of the clients. According to the building permit which Wright signed, this house (designed in 1916) was built in 1917. The builder was Hanney & Son. An article in the local paper discussed plans for a good-sized development of these houses, though it never materialized. Many historians have noted that this system failed to take off because of the US's involvement in the First World War. Oscar A Johnson, who has previously been thought to have been one of the first owners of the house, is not listed at this address between 1917 and 1925.   c95

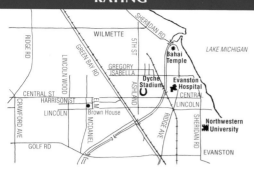

CHARLES A BROWN HOUSE
2420 Harrison Street
Evanston, Illinois 60201
1905 0503

GPS: N 42 03.790
W 87 42.458
UTM: 16 T 044 1453
456 5703

Directions: Harrison Street is parallel to and one block south of Central Street. Harrison is one way westbound on the 2400 block. Turn south off Central onto Elm for one block and west onto Harrison. The house is on the south side of the street, second from the west end of the block.

Accessibility: The front of the house can be seen from the street.

■ The story is that this was to be the prototype for a series of similar houses in a development. It is apparent from local directories that Mr Brown never lived in the house. Brown sold the property to John Chapin in September 1906.

There is another nearly identical house several blocks east, at 815 Lincoln. W Pierson of Adams & Westlake owned the property in 1907 and then sold it to Joseph C Kincaid, a decorator.

A further design was produced by Wright for a Royal H Jurgenson, which was exhibited in 1940. Nothing can be found relating to Jurgenson or his family in any city or phone directory of this period.   c96

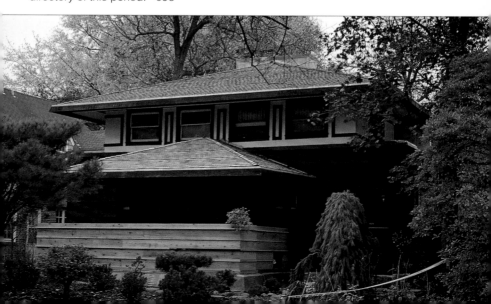

AW HEBERT HOUSE
1014 Hinman Street
Evanston, Illinois
1902 0112

GPS: N 42 04.719
       W 87 41.642
UTM: 16 T 044 2592
       465 8742

Directions: The house is on Hinman, which runs parallel to Chicago, between Dempster Street to the north and Main Street to the south. It is on the west side of the street.

Accessibility: The house is visible from the street.

■ The house was remodeled from an earlier building. Dr Hebert was a dentist who owned fifteen or more Evanston properties. The story goes that Wright and his family had dental work done by Hebert and that some of the remodeling was carried out as partial repayment of that debt. Hebert was the uncle of John H Howe, Wright's chief draftsman from 1932 until 1959. Howe provided most of this information to the author. There are drawings at the Taliesin Archive that detail most of the work that Wright did for this building. After a fire, most of what could be seen from the street was lost. c95

(Hebert was the architect for two of his own properties, 918 and 1012 Hinman Street. Constructed in 1894, number 1012 may have been his first venture in design. A private hotel at 1824 Hinman, now demolished, was the home of the architect and popular writer Thomas Tallmadge.)

AW HEBERT PROPERTIES

1300-02 Davis Street
1902
■ This property, pictured below, was already a well-designed Queen Anne duplex when it was remodeled by Wright and Walter Burley Griffin. The roofs were rebuilt and extensive work was done on the interior making it far more open and light than the original construction. (No 1306 Davis, also owned by Hebert, was not altered.)   c96

1713 Asbury Avenue
1902
■ Wright's work on this property was mostly to the interior. Across the street is Walter Burley Griffin's Bovee Duplex. Behind, facing Church Street, is the house that Wright's chief draftsman Jack Howe grew up in.

1308 Asbury Avenue
1902
■ There was less work carried out here than in the other Hebert properties. The most significant feature is the large concrete flower urn that perches on the second level at the south end of the façade. It is nearly six feet across and is a near duplicate of those for the Robie House (p125).

(Other Hebert properties include 918 (demolished about 1979), 1043,1045, 1049 and 1206 Hinman, the latter is very over grown and not easy to see. There is also one at 1119 Lake and a multi-family house at 1453 Ridge. Most of these buildings are covered in stucco. This material hides many additions and changes of exterior textures and materials. More research needs to be done on the Hebert and Howe families.)

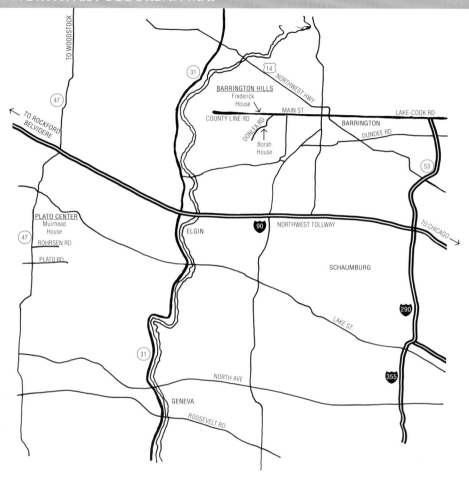

In the first half of this century most of the northwest suburbs were farmland, as they are today. There were no early population centers. For this reason, Wright's work in this area is widely scattered. It is grouped along the Interstate 90 that leads from Chicago to Madison, Wisconsin. The houses tend to be situated on building lots that are much larger than those of Chicago's other outlying regions. They are further from public ways and much more difficult, if not impossible, to see without an invitation from the residents.

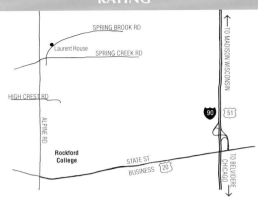

KENNETH LAURENT HOUSE
4646 Spring Brook Road
Rockford, Illinois 61111
1949 4814

GPS: N 42 17.266
        W 89 02.416

Directions: Exit Interstate 90 at New York westbound. Travel about 2 miles to Alpine and turn north for about 0.6 miles to Spring Creek. Spring Brook Road splits from Spring Creek to the northeast. The house is on the north side of the street.

Accessibility: The house cannot be seen from the road, approaching it will disturb the occupants.

■ Laurent is confined to a wheelchair. In general, Wright's Usonian houses, which tend to be on one level without any steps, are well suited to accommodating this disability. In the living room the brick wall is set back from the windows providing a wonderful panorama. The house is constructed from the soft, salmon-colored 'Chicago common' brick, which is often used as a backer or fill brick. Here, the color combines effectively with the plantings and the wood detailing. c77

PETTIT MEMORIAL CHAPEL
Harrison at Webster Street
Belvidere, Illinois 61008
1906 0619

GPS: N 42 16.153
       W 88 50.815

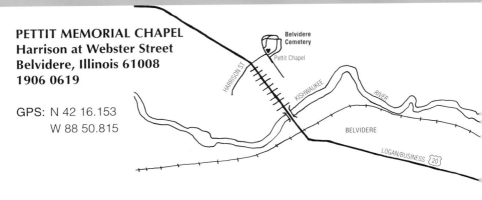

Directions: Exit Interstate 90 at Business Highway 20 and drive north to Logan. Take Logan west through town about 2 miles to Harrison. Turn north on Harrison for two blocks until it deadends at the entrance to the cemetery.

Accessibility: The chapel and cemetery are open during daylight hours.

■ The chapel had not been maintained well until it was restored during the early 1980s, in an early effort to recognize even the smallest of Wright's work. It has been a success and is certainly worth a visit. This building has an intimate almost residential feel to it, as opposed to more standard memorial structures. It is symmetrical on two sides unlike most of Wright's other work of the time. Emma Glasner Pettit was the sister of William A Glasner (see p33). Dr Pettit was a physician who worked in Iowa before moving to Belvidere. c77

ROBERT MUIRHEAD FARMHOUSE
Rohrsen Road
Plato Center, Illinois 60170
1950 5019

GPS: N 42 02.134
W 88 27.053

Directions: Exit Interstate 90 at Route 47, east of Rockford and Belvidere. Drive south 6.5 miles to Rohrsen Road, north of Plato Road. Continue east on Rohrsen for 2 miles. The house is only approached by driving under the viaduct.

Accessibility: The house cannot be approached without disturbing the occupants.

■ Though it looks like a very large and elaborate house, it is very compact with little extra room. It has the distinction of being the only farmhouse Wright designed. It is across the driveway from the original farmhouse, which had been added onto several times before the decision was made to build a new one. The drawings were completed in February 1951 with construction beginning the following summer. The same materials are used here as in the Laurent House (p43) – cypress and 'Chicago common' brick. It has heating pipes under the concrete floor.   c81

LOUIS B FREDERICK HOUSE
28 W 248 County Line Road
Barrington Hills, Illinois 60010
1954 5426

GPS: N 42 13.677
     W 88 08.452
UTM: 16 T 040 5853
     467 5716

Directions: Countyline Road is the border between Lake and Cook Counties and is called Lake-Cook Road further east in Highland Park. The Frederick House is near the eastern border of Barrington Hills. It is 2.6 miles west of Barrington Road. The house is noted by its mailbox and is on the north side of the street just over the top of a small hill up the driveway.

Accessibility: The house cannot be seen from the street.

■ In this case, Wright came to the clients and met them at Chicago's Blackstone Hotel on Michigan Avenue. They approached Wright after seeing the Exhibition House on the site of the future Guggenheim Building (Opus# 5314) (East volume). The playroom is down its own hall over 30 feet from the living room. Frederick was employed by the famous furniture and design store 'Colbys' in Chicago.   c95

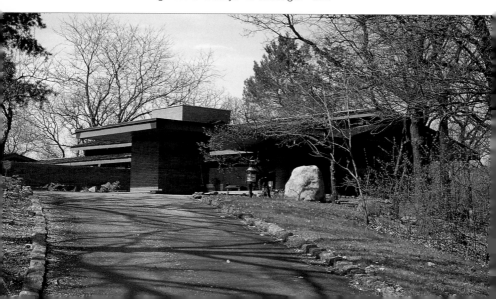

AL BORAH HOUSE
(Erdman Prefab #1)
265 Donlea Road
Barrington Hills, Illinois 60010
1957 5518

GPS: N 42 08.837
W 88 11.654
UTM: 16 T 040 1324
466 6819

Directions: Donlea Road is perpendicular to Countyline Road and intersects it just east of the Frederick House, 2.2 miles west of Barrington Road. Drive south for 0.8 miles and around a few curves. The house is on the east side of the street at the south shore of a large pond.

Accessibility: The house is some distance from the street but can be seen from it.

■ This house is called the Al Borah House after its builder. Borah, however, never lived in it. It was used as an exhibition house for the National Association of Home Builders (NAHB) for the 1958 Chicago Convention. As with all the Erdman Prefabs, this one was loaded on several flat-bed trucks and shipped from Madison, Wisconsin, to its site, then assembled. The site is perhaps the best of any Erdman Prefab, situated on a small lake in a district that requires the lots to be no less than 5 acres. Horses are allowed on these blocks of land. The house's first resident was Frederick B Post, who bought the house after the exhibit concluded.   c95

JOHN O CARR HOUSE
1544 Portage Run
Glenview, Illinois 60025
1950 5014

GPS: N 42 05.029
W 87 51.381
UTM: 16 T 042 9172
465 9437

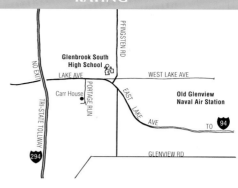

Directions: Turn off Lake Avenue south on to Portage Run and drive for about about half a mile. The house is on the west side of the street and is difficult to see through all the trees. The Baker House (p36) is on Lake Avenue several miles to the east.

Accessibility: The house is very difficult to see in both summer and winter because of the profusion of small trees and shrubs. There is an electric eye across the driveway that alerts the occupants to anyone approaching the house.

■ A rare publication, *Taliesin Drawings,* features a beautiful rendition of this house. Unfortunately, the house has had additions that reduce the clarity and cohesion of the smaller, simpler original design. Mr Carr only lived in the house a short time. c96

  (In the northwest suburb is also the site of the Park Ridge Country Club, which was built in 1912 and demolished in the 1930s, Opus #1204. Like the Booth House, on p26, it combined two previously separate buildings. A flat-roofed line of wings and pergolas connected the two pavilions to create a dance floor.)

EDWARD C WALLER HOUSE SITE
Auvergne Place
River Forest, Illinois 60305
1899 9902

Directions: Waller's estate was east of the Des Plaines River (just east of First Avenue) and north of Lake Street. It extended about three blocks east to Edgewood and one long block north. The estate is and was entered through the Wright-designed gates at Auvergne Place, as Waller named it. The Waller House was northwest of the still existing Winslow House.

Accessibility: The estate can be seen, although it was subdivided in the 1960s.

■ Waller was born in 1845 in Kentucky and moved to Chicago in 1860. There were three other prominent Waller families from Kentucky, one of them also came to Chicago in the same year. It is not known if they were related. In 1866, at the age of twenty-one, he founded a real-estate firm. A Rebecca H Waller bought this land in 1880 and deeded it to John D Waller in 1882. It is not known if these Wallers were related to Edward or the other Waller families from Kentucky. Edward purchased the property in January 1886. He was a lifelong friend of Daniel Burnham, who was the original designer of his house. Waller arranged the 1894 meeting between Burnham and Wright, enabling Burnham to offer Wright a position in his firm as chief designer. The story goes that Burnham had been greatly impressed by Wright's fine design work on Blossom House (p123). From the dean of American architecture at that time, this was not something to be scoffed at and would have overwhelmed most architects. Wright, however, rejected the offer stating that he was already spoiled by the success of his own work.

The original Waller House designed by Burnham was a restrained Victorian dwelling. It was a compact composition that did not include towers, turrets and other fancywork. A long, curved walkway led to a large greenhouse to the south of the east facing house – a large building, it was built to supply the estate with fruit and vegetables.

Waller's involvement in real estate made him an important client for Wright and other Chicago architects. He was responsible for the Burnham & Root-desgned building, The Rookery (p135), where Wright and the Luxfer Prism Co had offices; he was an original stockholder in the Luxfer Prism Co. He was also behind the Cheltenham Beach Project at 79th Street and the lakefront, Midway Gardens, the Waller Apartments, Francisco Terrace and many others. Waller was founder and president of the Central Safety Deposit Company, which built William Le Baron Jenney's Home Insurance Company Building, the first steel-framed building. Waller owned thousands of acres at Charlevoix, Michigan (see UGL volume), and had Wright design several buildings for that property. Only one, a bathing pavilion, was built. In the *Book of Chicagoans*, he listed his recreations as farming and golf. Many of Wright's clients were avid golfers and belonged to exclusive clubs in the Chicago area. The house was demolished in 1939, a few years after Waller's death in 1930, and the stables some time afterwards.

NORTH AVE

RIVER FOREST

HARLEM AVE

DES PLAINES RIVER

THATCHER AVE

Walter Gale House
Thomas Gale House
Parker House

Balch House

WOODBINE

FOREST AVE

Frank Lloyd Wright
Home & Studio

CHICAGO AVE

Roberts House

EDGEWOOD PLACE

KEYSTONE

OAK

Wooley House
Hills House
Moore House

ASH LAND

LATHROP AVE

River Forest
Tennnis Club

QUICK ST

BONNIE BRAE

Beachy House

MARION

AUVERGNE PLACE

Ingalls
House

Thomas
House

DES PLAINES RIVER

1ST AVE

Winslow House

Williams House

LAKE ST

Davenport House

HOME

George Smith
House

MADISON ST

TO

290

HARLEM AVE

TO

290

RIVERSIDE
Coonley House
Tomek House
Coonley Playhouse

■ About a third of all of Wright's existing buildings in the MetroChicago area are located in Oak Park and River Forest. They are all situated within the boundaries of 1st Avenue on the west and Austin Boulevard on the east (the western border of Chicago), North Avenue (Route 64) on the north and Jackson Boulevard on the south. The boundary line between the two suburbs is Harlem Avenue. These two areas are north of Interstate 290, Eisenhower Expressway, that goes west from downtown Chicago to Elmhurst.

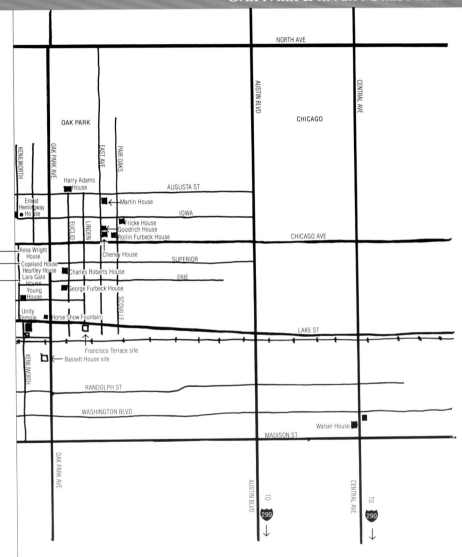

NORTH AVE

AUSTIN BLVD

CENTRAL AVE

OAK PARK

CHICAGO

KENILWORTH

OAK PARK AVE

EAST AVE

PAIR OAKS

Harry Adams
House

AUGUSTA ST

Ernest
Hemingway
House

Martin House

IOWA

EUCLID

LINDEN

Fricke House
Goodrich House
Rollin Furbeck House

CHICAGO AVE

Anna Wright
House
Copeland House
Heurtley House
Lara Gale
House
Young
House

Cheney House

SUPERIOR

Charles Roberts House

ERIE

George Furbeck House

SCOVILLE

Unity
Temple

Horse Show Fountain

LAKE ST

KENILWORTH

Francisco Terrace site

Bassett House site

RANDOLPH ST

WASHINGTON BLVD

Walser House

MADISON ST

OAK PARK AVE

AUSTIN BLVD

TO 290

CENTRAL AVE

TO 290

River Forest was incorporated in 1880 and Oak Park in 1902. The first paving stones were laid in the streets of Oak Park in 1889 and by 1900 there were street cars. Most of the town had access to a central-heating system that was designed and installed by Yarrian. It was steam heated, which accounts for most of the early Wright works having radiators instead of the gravity heating found in many of the building's of Wright's first employer Joseph Lyman Silsbee.

WILLIAM HERMAN WINSLOW HOUSE
515 Auvergne Place
River Forest, Illinois 60305
1894 9305

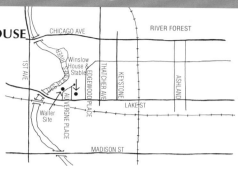

GPS: N 41 53.327
      W 87 49.747
UTM: 16 T 043 1205
      463 7764

Directions: The house is in River Forest just north of Lake Street and east of both 1st Avenue and the Des Plaines River bridge into River Forest.

Accessibility: The front of the house can be seen from the street.

■ Winslow was born in Brooklyn in 1857. In 1881 he worked for Hecla Iron Works in New York, as did the art glass supplier Orlando Giannini and Giannini's brother. William and his brother came to Chicago the same year as the two Gianninis. Winslow Brothers Iron Works on west Carroll Street produced the decorative metalwork for Daniel Burnham's Rookery (p135) and Louis Sullivan's Carson, Pirie, Scott buildings. William Winslow married Edith Henry of St Louis in 1891. The property was bought on 1 November 1894 from John D Waller, no apparent relation of Edward C. Winslow's patronage gave Wright the opportunity to produce his first substantial work when he was only twenty-four.

Winslow's property is on the former estate of Edward Waller. No one is sure of how the house came to be built within the gates of the estate, but Winslow lived here until his death in the 1930s. c79

The dichotomy of the simple street façade and the more complex rear of the house is a result of Wright's design methods. The house was planned and then the floor plan was made to fit. Wright did this with many of his houses before he began to design in total in about 1900. The classical base-column-capital motif demonstrates the extent to which Wright understood classicism and the design tenents of the time. It was his manipulation of a given language that made his work so outstanding – familiar with a twist. Today it is difficult to date this design, it looks as if it could have been built some sixty years later .

When first built, the house was monochromatic. The roof and the frieze nearly matched the color of the brick. The limestone trim was not painted white. The trim around the front door, however, is much more severe and abstract than both the plaster frieze, which surrounds the second story, and the oak carving on the top of the front entry door.

Winslow was very interested in music and played the violin. He was an inventor and liked to be involved in many activities. He had a printing press called the 'Auvergne Press'. He was responsible for printing the first edition of the classic, *The House Beautiful* in 1896, written by Wright's uncle's friend William Gannett. Wright designed the elaborate page borders and assisted in the three-year printing effort. Winslow and his across-the-yard neighbor, Chauncey Williams, were also involved in printing John Keats' *Eve of St Agnes*. Winslow invented the system that made the Luxfer Prism system workable and was one of the original incorporators along with Waller and William MacHarg (p114).

There was a very tall wooden toboggan slide on the north side of the house for the amusement of the neighborhood children. According to several historians, the stable in the backyard may have been designed and built a few years after the house. Winslow moved his printing press to one of the south rooms of the stable block from its original location in the basement of the house. Many years ago the stable building was converted into a separate residence.

CHAUNCEY L WILLIAMS HOUSE
530 Edgewood Place
River Forest, Illinois 60305
1895 9505

GPS: N 41 53.334
W 87 49.652

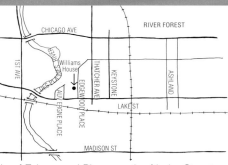

Directions: The house is on the west side of Edgewood Place north of Lake Street.

Accessibility: The front of the house can be seen from the street.

■ The house was scaled to accommodate Williams's height: he was six feet four inches tall. With money inherited from his father, Williams started a publishing firm Way & Williams. He knew attorney Clarence Darrow and Kansas Governor Henry J Allen (see West volume) along with bookseller George Millard (p22), who were all Wright clients. Williams bought the land from Waller in May 1895. He lived there only until 1903 when his business went bust and he moved to a house nearby. The house is reported to have a Giannini mural that may now be overpainted. Williams had an interest in the Turner Brass Works for whom Giannini produced an important poster design. Williams is meant to have been an integral part of the Wright/Waller/Winslow circle. The large rocks set into the masonry at the entry were taken from the nearby Des Plaines River on Waller's estate.

The original dormers were replaced in 1901, although one survives on the north side at the back of the house. The library is the octagonal room to the left of the front door. A window on the front at the north end has been filled in. c75

ISABEL ROBERTS HOUSE
603 Edgewood Place
River Forest, Illinois 60305
1908 0808

GPS: N 41 53.891
W 87 49.570

Directions: The Roberts House is north of the Williams House on Edgewood, next door to William Drummond's own house and across from another Drummond design.

Accessibility: The house can be seen from the street.

■ A similar design was first proposed for JG Melson of Mason City, Iowa, a few years earlier. It must have caught Miss Roberts's eye while she was the secretary/book-keeper in Wright's office. Miss Roberts helped Herman von Holst while Wright was in Europe from 1909 to 1911. The house had a full set of Wright-designed furniture most of which still survives, though not *in situ*. It was built on land owned by Isabel's mother, Mary, just east of Waller's property.

In the 1950s subsequent owners, who got into trouble remodeling the house, asked Wright for his assistance. The interior was updated with mahogany built-in cabinetry in the dining room and lapped boards replacing the banded ceiling in the living room. The entry was altered and the exterior stucco was bricked over. This interior is the only Prairie design to be updated by Wright. It shows just how well his designs stand the test of time.   c74

J KIBBEN INGALLS HOUSE
562 Keystone Avenue
River Forest, Illinois 60305
1909 0906

Directions: The Ingalls House is on the first block north of Lake Street on Keystone Avenue. It is on the west side of the street.

Accessibility: The front of the house can be seen from the street.

■ Born in 1870, Ingalls was self-educated and a book collector of Western Americana. He worked for Western Heater Dispatch, which heated and later cooled railroad box cars. In the 1920s his Northwestern Refrigerator Line Co, which built refrigerated units, was sold to the North American Car Co. Ingalls died in 1937 and his widow continued to live in the house until about 1950 when she passed away. His grandson later founded the architectural bookstore, Hennessey & Ingalls, in Santa Monica, California.

This is one of the few symmetrical buildings after the Winslow and Hoyt Houses (pp52 and 95). The entry here is on the front facing the street. It has been said that Ingalls required Wright to give each room three exposures to allow maximum light and ventilation. William Drummond made several alterations in 1917 and 1926. c75

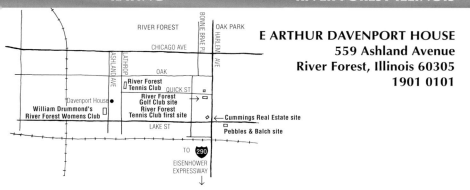

E ARTHUR DAVENPORT HOUSE
559 Ashland Avenue
River Forest, Illinois 60305
1901 0101

Directions: The house is in the first block north of Lake Street on Ashland on the east side of the street.

Accessibility: The front of the house can be seen from the street.

■ Davenport worked for The Pullman Company for fifty-two years, though he was not required to live in the town of Pullman, now part of Chicago. This was one of a few houses designed by Wright in partnership with another architect, Webster Tomlinson. The original house (see p147) was later dramatically remodeled when its square porch and octagonal bay protected with a roof overhang were removed. It was very similar to 'A Small House with Lots of Room in It' published in the *Ladies Home Journal* of July 1901. In 1911, Tomlinson designed a summer cottage for the Davenports. c74

RIVER FOREST TENNIS CLUB
615 Lathrop Avenue
River Forest, Illinois 60305
1906 0510

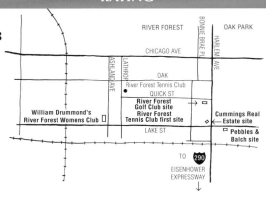

Directions: The tennis club is on the first block north of Lake Street on Lathrop Avenue. It is on the east side of the street.

Accessibility: The front of the building can be seen from the street.

■   The original building was constructed on land at Harlem Avenue and Quick Street and completed on 4 July 1905. After it perished in a fire, this building was constructed in 1906, in a single month, at a cost of $2,629.75. In 1920, it was sawn into three parts and moved by horse to its present location. It has had several additions, making it a bit of a hodge podge. The graphic rendered in metal and set on the front of the brick chimney may be a Wright design (see photograph below).   c96

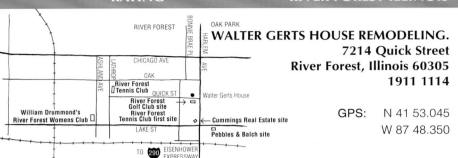

WALTER GERTS HOUSE REMODELING.
7214 Quick Street
River Forest, Illinois 60305
1911 1114

GPS: N 41 53.045
                W 87 48.350

Directions: The Gerts House is on Quick Street just west of Harlem Avenue. Quick is one-way eastbound and can only be approached from Bonnie Brae; the house is one block north of Lake Street.

Accessibility: The front of the house can be seen from the street.

■ This house was designed by Charles E White in 1905 on a block that also contained a Tallmadge & Watson and a great Guenzel & Drummond four-square. Wright remodeled it after a fire. Walter Gerts also had a summer house designed by Wright (see UGL volume). Mrs Gerts and Mrs Laura Robeson Gale (see pp61 and 71) were sisters.   c96

(The River Forest Golf Club was built in 1898, Opus# 9802, with additions in 1901, Opus #0105, and demolished in 1905. A small nine-hole course at Bonnie Brae and Quick, to the south of the Gerts House, it was later the site of the first River Forest Tennis Club and at the southeast corner, the Cummings Real Estate Office. Built in 1907, Opus #0702, the office was demolished in the 1920s. It was at the northwest corner of Lake Street and Harlem Avenue. Cummings gave the land to the Forest Preserve District.)

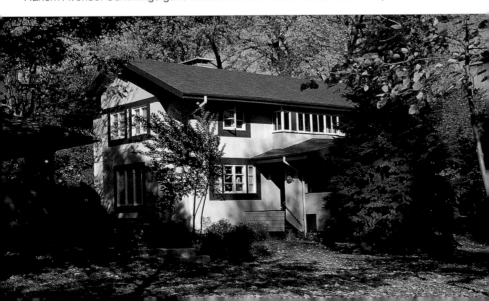

WALTER M GALE HOUSE
1031 Chicago Avenue
Oak Park, Illinois 60302
1893 9302

Directions: Exit Interstate 290 at Harlem Avenue and drive north for a mile to Chicago Avenue. The house is between the Thomas Gale House on the east and a commercial building on the west, on the south side of Chicago Avenue.

Accessibility: The house can be seen from the street.

■ In October 1891, Edwin O Gale sold his six residential lots on Chicago Avenue to his son, Thomas. By 6 June 1892, Solon S Beman and his wife Fanny bought this lot. In October 1893, Beman sold the property back to the Gales to Thomas's brother, Walter. A bachelor, Walter Gale was a druggist in downtown Chicago.

The construction of this house was begun by architect LD Beman, in the spring of 1893, for Charles Mortimer. Work had not got far when Gale bought it and had Wright design the house as it is today (AS). The spindle railing and open porch are unique to Wright's early work. Most of the Prairie buildings had porches with roofs, which were integrated into the buildings. This architectural element may have been included to balance the geometry of the existing foundations. Walter Gale sold the property in March 1906.   c74

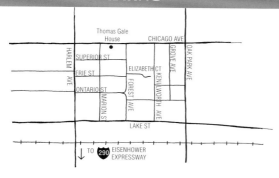

THOMAS H GALE HOUSE
1027 Chicago Avenue
Oak Park, Illinois 60302
1892 9203

Directions: There is a series of three Wright-designed houses on Chicago Avenue, a couple of blocks east of Harlem Avenue past the small commercial district. The houses are located on the south side of the street.

Accessibility: The front of the house can be seen from the street.

■ Born in 1866, Thomas Gale met his wife Laura while they were both students at the University of Michigan. Wright knew Gale through Unity Church. The houses are a variation on a popular Queen Anne style with a two-story bay topped by a turret. Thomas Gale was a realtor with offices in the Oxford Building. After buying the lots along Chicago Avenue from his father, Thomas sold all of them within the next two years. The lots were 50 feet wide and 183 feet deep. The Gales sold this property to Annie Anderson in October 1897, and the Andersons sold it again in 1901.   c77

    Thomas Gale's wife, Laura, built another Wright-designed house after Thomas's death in 1908 on nearby Elizabeth Court (p71).

ROBERT P PARKER HOUSE
1019 Chicago Avenue
Oak Park, Illinois 60302
1892 9206

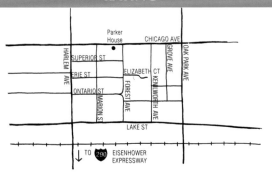

Directions: This house is the second east of the Thomas Gale House on Chicago Avenue.

Accessibility: The front of the house can be seen from the street

■ This house was built speculatively by Thomas Gale (p61). Parker, an attorney, must have bought it before construction began, in May 1892, as his name is on the drawings. Parker, however, did not live in the house very long. In November 1895, he sold it to William S Harvey. Not much is known about Parker or his family. If the family could be found, perhaps there would be family photographs of what the interior looked like while Parker lived here. The historian Paul Sprague has suggested to me that the design is based on the earlier Emmond House (p104) for La Grange.   c77

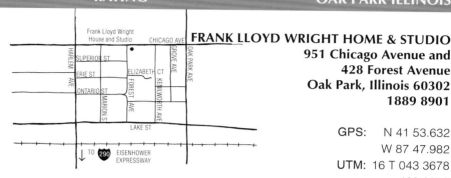

FRANK LLOYD WRIGHT HOME & STUDIO
951 Chicago Avenue and
428 Forest Avenue
Oak Park, Illinois 60302
1889 8901

GPS:	N 41 53.632
	W 87 47.982
UTM:	16 T 043 3678
	463 8318

Directions: The studio is three blocks west of Harlem Avenue on Chicago Avenue, at the corner of Forest Avenue.

Accessibility: Everyday there are regular tours of the home and studio. Call 708/848-1976 for more information. Some of these tours include Forest Avenue and Unity Temple. There is a special tour on the third Saturday in May every year called 'Wright Plus.' This day includes tours of the neighborhood and the interiors of several significant buildings in Oak Park, and occasionally nearby River Forest.

■ Wright must have loved designing houses, he worked on more than a thousand of them. This was his first house, which he built for his family. Many alterations followed, but the most significant additions were the kitchen and playroom of 1895 and the studio of 1897 facing Chicago Avenue, the commercial street.   c96

Although Wright did not marry until 1 June 1889, he bought the vacant land on 5 May 1889 for $2,875 from Jane and John Blair, residents of British Columbia in Canada, and listed himself as married on the deed. Wright was working for Adler & Sullivan at this time and was able to borrow $5,000 from Louis Sullivan, personally, by a contract dated 17 August 1889. Sullivan then got a mortgage from Henry Austin on 20 August for $2,150. (For further details of this loan see pp11-12.)

The integration of home and studio reflected Wright's involvement with the Arts and Crafts philosophy advocated by the English architect William Morris. Henry Hobson Richardson's architectural office and the workshops of the Roycrofters' Elbert Hubbard in New York also adopted a similar approach. Architecture was meant to be a part of an artist or craftsman's life, to be practised throughout the week. There was no separation between office and home life. Wright lived architecture twenty-four hours a day. His family and children were frequently present in the drafting room during office hours and he was often there at weekends and during the evenings.

When Wright moved out of the family home in 1911, he remodeled these buildings into apartments and living quarters for his estranged wife, Catherine, and their children. The extra apartment provided an income for Catherine and helped offset living expenses. Later, Clyde Nooker owned the property and maintained it very well until his widow sold it to the Frank Lloyd Wright Home and Studio Foundation in 1974. In the mid-1950s, Wright was called in by the Nookers to carry out some minor remodeling for them. These alterations with any other changes made after 1909 have now been removed. The year 1909 was chosen because it was the last year that Wright used the house and studio as they were originally intended. Now owned by the National Park Service and a National Trust Property, they are managed by the Frank Lloyd Wright Home and Studio Foundation.

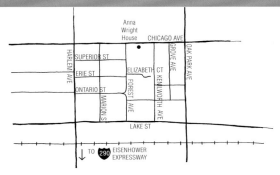

ANNA L WRIGHT HOUSE
(now headquarters for the
Frank Lloyd Wright Home
and Studio Foundation)
931 West Chicago Avenue
Oak Park, Illinois 60301

Directions: The house is behind a shingled fence on Chicago Avenue, east of Wright's studio.

Accessibility: The exterior of the house can be seen from the street.

■ On 27 July 1866, Jane and John Blair bought this property from Henry W Austin. By 1873, Blair, who was a landscape gardener, had built the house. He is probably responsible for the variety of trees on the site. Anna Lloyd Jones Wright moved here at the suggestion of Rev Chapin, a female Oak Park Unitarian minister. Anna bought the house from the Blairs on 21 August 1889, about two months after her son bought the western half of Lot 20. She purchased it for $3,200: the Blairs took back the mortgage in full plus an additional loan of $300, which was to be repaid at an interest rate of 7 per cent. Some work was done to the building, including the extension of the fence across the front on Chicago Avenue. After their wedding, Wright and Catherine moved in until their own house was completed next door. The house was known by Wright's children as 'Grandmother's Cottage.' Anna's daughter, Jane Porter, bought it in 1918 and sold it in 1922.   c96

WILLIAM H COPELAND HOUSE
400 Forest Avenue
Oak Park, Illinois 60302
1909 0904

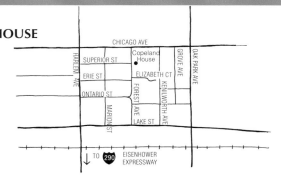

Directions: This house is fourth on Forest Avenue from the corner of Chicago Avenue, on the east side of the street.

Accessibility: The front of the house can be seen from the street.

■ William Harman built this house in the early 1870s. In December 1898 Copeland bought it and lived here until March 1929. The garage was built to Wright's plans in 1908 and in 1909 the house was remodeled by Wright (AS). On the interior we find the standard moldings and trim of the Prairie era. In this case the 11-foot ceiling heights are much greater than Wright's usual constructions. He compensates by adding two smaller trim pieces, which run parallel to the standard headband. These are similar to those in the much earlier Fricke House (p85). The result is not very satisfactory. It reminds us just how difficult and delicate good design really is, when well-proportioned details often appear to come so easily to Wright.   c96

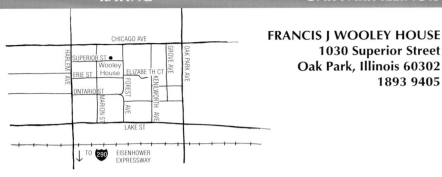

FRANCIS J WOOLEY HOUSE
1030 Superior Street
Oak Park, Illinois 60302
1893 9405

Directions: The Wooley House is south of and behind the Gale Houses on Chicago Avenue; it is on the north side of Superior Street just west of Moore House.

Accessibility: The house can be seen from the street.

■ Wooley was an attorney. The house is similar in layout to the Emmond and Gale Houses (pp60, 61 and 104), as well as the Parker House (p62), which is immediately north of the Wooley House. For many years the building had red-asphalt sidings, which were recently carefully removed exposing the original wood sidings. Wooley's son, Taylor, worked for Wright in the Oak Park Studio and in Fiesole, Italy, on the Wasmuth drawings in 1909 and 1910. Taylor later moved to Salt Lake City, set up practice and produced a group of very well-designed buildings there. His records are in the archives at a university in Salt Lake City. From city directories, it appears that Francis J Wooley had moved to Glencoe by at least 1903; he is listed there into the 1920s.   c96

NATHAN G MOORE HOUSE
333 Forest Avenue at Superior
Oak Park, Illinois 60302
1895 9503
(remodeling 1923 2303
pergola 1905 0527)

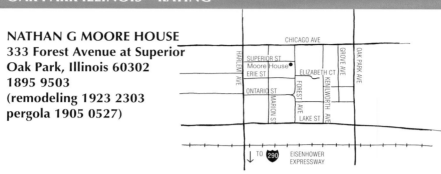

Directions: The Moore House is one block south of Chicago Avenue at the southwest corner of Superior Street and Forest Avenue.

Accessibility: The house can be seen from the street.

■ Born in Pennsylvania in 1853, Moore became a lawyer in Peoria before moving to Chicago. In 1894 he asked Wright to remodel the first house on this site but soon realized that it would be too small and asked for something 'Elizabethan.' The resulting house was imitated by architects for years to come. An example can be seen on Oak Park Avenue at Thomas Street and another as far away as Valladolid, near Cancun, Mexico.

On Christmas Day 1922, the top floor and roof of the house were destroyed by fire. Wright gained the commission as he happened to be in Chicago at the time and contacted Moore. Charles E White was Wright's local representative. The result was much more decorative than the earlier work. It included a considerable amount of terra cotta, taken from designs found in Louis Sullivan's buildings. How these came to be used here remains a mystery. West of the south yard are the original stable and garage.   c76

EDWARD R HILLS HOUSE
313 Forest Avenue
Oak Park, Illinois 60302
1906 0102

Directions: The Hills House is south of the Moore House.

Accessibility: The house can be seen from the street.

■ The house was built in 1883 by Charles C Miller for Frank S Gray, grandfather of William Gray Purcell of Purcell & Elmslie. The original stick-style house, which stood just to the north, was moved and turned 90 degrees to its present location. In March 1900, Nathan G Moore (see p68) bought the property. In 1906, he had it remodeled by Wright, according to plans drawn up in 1900, for his daughter and attorney husband, Hills. Hills acquired title to the property on 23 December 1910. After a fire in 1976, it was rebuilt according to Wright's drawings. The interior was updated and moldings introduced. Virtually everything above the floor of the first level is new. I was site superintendent for the reconstruction and wrote the story of the rebuilding on the house's framing members. The second-floor bay is suspended from trusses in the roof in the same manner as the balcony of the Jacobs II House in Middleton (UGL volume, p54). The original colors were grey stucco with green trim, similar to that of the Thomas House (p73).   c81

ARTHUR HEURTLEY HOUSE
318 Forest Avenue
Oak Park, Illinois 60302
1902 0204

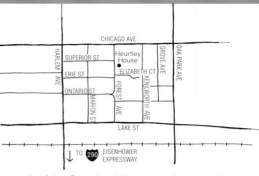

CHICAGO AVE
HARLEM AVE
SUPERIOR ST
Heurtley House
GROVE AVE
OAK PARK AVE
ERIE ST
ELIZABETH CT
ONTARIO ST
MARION ST
FOREST AVE
KENILWORTH AVE
LAKE ST
↓ TO 290 EISENHOWER EXPRESSWAY

Directions: The Heurtley House is south of the Copeland House and across the street from the Moore House on the east side of Forest Avenue.

Accessibility: The front of the house can be seen from the street.

■ Born in Boston in 1860, Heurtley was a banker for the Northern Trust Bank. After moving to Chicago in 1881, his interest in music led him to become the president of the Apollo Musical Society. He was also a member of the Cliff Dwellers' Club. Golf was a big part of his life and he was a member of one of the oldest golf clubs, Chicago Golf Club, in Wheaton. He was a member of Oak Park Country Club and the River Forest Tennis Club. He died at his summer house in Muscatane, Iowa, in 1934.

Heurtley bought this property in March 1902 and in the same year commissioned Wright to remodel his cottage on Marquette Island at the exclusive Les Cheneaux Club at Cedarville, Michigan (UGL volume, p98). In 1920, Wright's brother-in-law, Andrew T Porter, purchased the house. Porter removed all the original furniture to Tan-y-Deri in Spring Green (UGL volume, p48).   c81

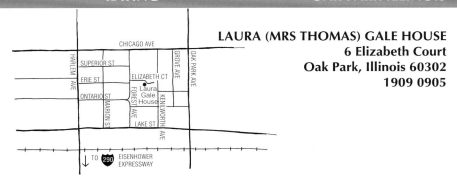

LAURA (MRS THOMAS) GALE HOUSE
6 Elizabeth Court
Oak Park, Illinois 60302
1909 0905

Directions: Just one house further south of the Heurtley House is a short street, Elizabeth Court. It is now only accessible by car from Forest Avenue, but on foot can be approached from either direction. Elizabeth Court is the only street in Oak Park with a curve in it. The street is named after the wife of a former Oak Park mayor. This block has its own numbering system. The house is on the south side of the street just east of the curve.

Accessibility: The house can be seen from the street.

■ The art glass windows act as screens rather than barriers, protecting from the weather while enhancing the view (AS). Walter Gale bought the lot from Elizabeth Humphry on 11 January 1907 and sold it to his brother Thomas on 16 January. When Thomas Gale died later that year, his wife Laura employed Wright to design a house for her on a limited budget. This was rare as few clients have used Wright's services more than once. Laura lived in the house until her death in 1943. This is one of the smallest lots in Oak Park, just north of the Beachy House garage.   c75

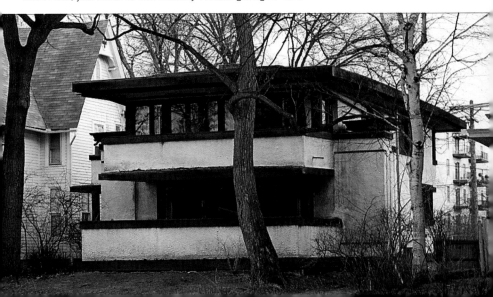

PETER A BEACHY HOUSE
238 Forest Avenue
Oak Park, Illinois 60302
1906 0601

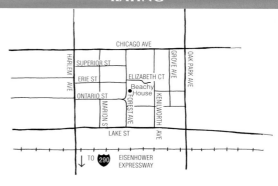

Directions: The Beachy House is in the center of the second block south of Chicago Avenue on the east side of Forest Avenue.

Accessibility: The house can be seen from the street.

■ Born in 1859, Beachy was a banker, who lived until he was ninety. He was related to Robert Blacker of Greene & Greene fame of Pasadena, California.

    Originally the commission was to remodel an existing house. Ultimately, this structure was consumed by the additions. The first house was a modest Victorian cottage built by a Mr Fargo. The Beachy House is one of the largest residential privately owned lots in Oak Park. The wishes of the client are evident here in two respects: there is no art glass and the scale is much larger than most other Prairie buildings. One end of the garage was used for the chauffeur and the other as a laboratory for Beachy's experiments. The house has seven gables.   c96

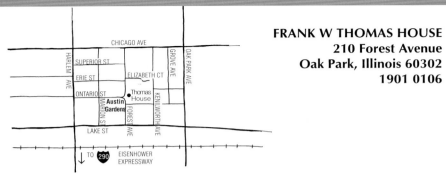

FRANK W THOMAS HOUSE
210 Forest Avenue
Oak Park, Illinois 60302
1901 0106

Directions: The house is two south of the Beachy House at the intersection of Forest Avenue and Ontario Street. It is across the street from Austin Gardens, the site of one of the earliest residents and now the location of summer Shakespeare programs.

Accessibility: The house comes right up to the sidewalk.

■ Thomas was born in 1870 in Ohio. He tried banking before becoming a stock broker for Slaughter & Co at the Chicago Board of Trade, where he became a partner in 1903. The house was a wedding present from his father-in-law, James C Rodgers – the drawings are in Rodgers' name. This is the first of Wright's Prairie Style houses and follows his definition of the style: no basement, no attic, living rooms on the second level and sets of in-line windows. The raised living rooms catch the breezes and give privacy to the occupants. The dazzling art glass incorporates mirrored gold glass accents, though in some places it is obscured by the storm windows. The entry is through the arch and up to the left, doubling back to the right and through a glass room surrounded by full-height art glass doors. c78

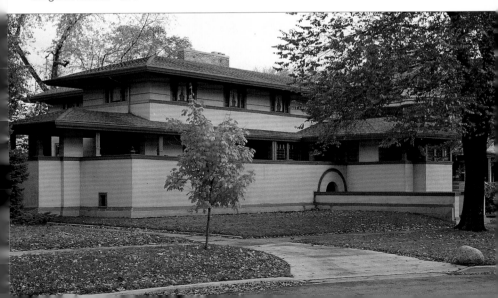

OAK PARK SITES

LEO BRAMSON DRESS SHOP SITE, Lake Street,
Oak Park, Illinois 60302
1937 3706

■ This dress shop was to have had a glass entry set back from the adjacent store fronts. There was a second-floor and third-floor balcony. This design would have brought the trendy Moderne style to the main street of Oak Park. It was among the first works of Wright's renaissance along with the Johnson Wax Building and Fallingwater. A drawing of the shop appears in Arthur Drexler's book on Wright drawings.

PEBBLES & BALCH SHOP SITE, 1107 (was 144) Lake Street,
Oak Park, Illinois 60302
1907 0708

■ The first-floor remodeling of this existing frame building on the south side of Lake Street made Wright's presence felt in the commercial district of his own home town. Pebbles was noted as a portrait painter and lived on Erie Street in Oak Park. Leo Bramson moved his dress shop to this location after the first tenants moved. The building was demolished during the 1940s.

Wright designed a house for Balch several years later (see p80). Carla Lind (*Lost Wright*, Simon & Schuster, New York, 1996) has found that between 1934 and 1940 Mrs Pebbles had a small restaurant designed by Wright called the Blue Patio, which was at 1120 Westgate, at the back of the shop.

DR HW BASSETT HOUSE SITE, 125 South Oak Park Avenue,
Oak Park, Illinois 60302
1894 9402

■ In 1922, the Bassett House was demolished to make way for a new commercial building that stands on its site today. Bassett was a homeopathic physician and had Wright remodel his house to include a small office area. He did not, however, live here long; he probably moved away in about 1900. Previously the house was the boyhood home of Walter Burley Griffin, from at least 1885 when the city directories began; Griffin, who was apprenticed to Wright, went on to plan and design much of Canberra, Australia. His father, George Walter Griffin, sold the house to Bassett. Griffin attended Oak Park High School and would have seen the work on his former home. This may have been the first contact between Wright and Griffin. The house was first published in May 1978 in the *Frank Lloyd Wright Newsletter*. No photographs have been found of the building before the Wright remodeling.

UNITY TEMPLE
861 Lake Street
at Kenilworth Avenue
Oak Park, Ill.
1906 0611

Directions: Unity Temple is at the corner of Lake Street and Kenilworth Avenue, one block east of Forest Avenue and two blocks south of Chicago Avenue. It is two blocks east of Harlem Avenue and one block north of the Lake Street 'L' line and the Northwestern train tracks. It is east of the Oak Park Post Office.

Accessibility: The temple can be seen from outside and there are tours of the interior on a regular basis. Contact 708/383-8873 and 708/848-1500 for the Oak Park Visitors' Center .

■ The original Gothic revival church was destroyed by fire in June 1905. In its place, the temple was built with a budget of $45,000. Built by Unitarians, who still practise there, it differs from other churches in its use of imagery, as they do not adopt the conventional Christian symbolism of the cross or in architecture the spire.

    Construction started in 1906 and was completed by 1908. It was built on a block bounded on the north by a noisy street car and on the south by two train lines. The high windows help keep the noise to a minimum, while also providing ventilation for the build-

up of hot air rising from below. The two similar but unequal blocks – 'Unity Temple' for worship and 'Unity House' for social-service functions – are joined by a low entry link that contains the church office on a second level. On the temple side, no seat is more than 45 feet from the pulpit. It remains a transcendent work bound to the earth and open to the heavens (AS).

Stand across the street and look at the base of the building. Imagine a point at the top of a person's head who is about 6 feet tall. Where would that point be? Now, go over to the base and see where it meets your own proportions. One is nearly always surprised at the changes in scale at Unity Temple. From some places, it appears very large and from others, smaller.

The complete history of this building has only recently been fully researched by Joseph Siry (see *Unity Temple*, Cambridge University Press, 1996). He has begun to explain the integration of the engineering, load transfers, cantilevers and beams to show how Wright integrated them, enhancing the appearance of the building both inside and out. Most buildings hide their engineering but Unity Temple exalts it, though not in a 'let it all hang out' way. The walls are braced by the balconies and the roof is held up by the tall square box that hides the pyramidal weather skylight and the interior waffle grid that allows light through the ceiling. The heating comes through the hollow columns at the four corners of the auditorium space. The wood bands often lap the concrete expansion joints. Entering around the side through the back stairs and exiting past the podium is a well-planned circulation route.

(The TE Gilpin House, Opus #0514, was reported to have been built nearby at North Boulevard and Kenilworth Avenue. Gilpin was the manager of Cicero Lumber Co and lived at 115 North Kenilworth in 1903. No evidence, however, has come to light to suggest that Wright's design was ever constructed.)

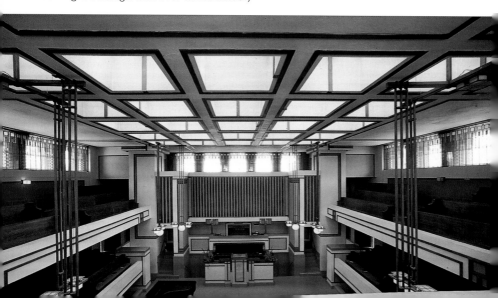

HORSE SHOW ASSOCIATION FOUNTAIN
(Scoville Park Fountain)
Lake Street and Oak Park Avenue
Oak Park, Illinois 60302
1909 0305

Directions: At the northwest corner of Lake Street and Oak Park Avenue

Accessibility: Full access is available at all times and conditions in Scoville Park.

■ Commissioned by the Horse Show Association, the fountain was designed by Richard Bock with Wright only suggesting the opening in the middle (AS). Formerly located west at the center of the block on Lake Street, it was intended to supply refreshment for man and beast. Charles E Roberts (see p87) was part of the committee and was photographed with Bock at the dedication. The existing reconstructed structure is not exactly as it was designed and originally built.   c96

GEORGE W SMITH HOUSE
404 South Home Avenue
Oak Park, Illinois 60302
1896 9803

Directions: The Smith House is outside the concentration of other Wright-designed buildings and the only one south of the railroad tracks. It is three blocks east of Harlem Avenue and one block north of Madison on Home Avenue. Home Avenue is in the same line with Forest Avenue but the name changes at the Lake Street 'L' tracks.

Accessibility: The front of the house can be seen from the street.

■ The walls are broken into the sort of rectangular planes which are more common to detailing in stucco than shingle (AS). The double-pitch roof is characteristic of Myron Hunt, an Evanston architect who like Wright worked in Joseph Lyman Silsbee's office. Until Smith's family come forward we will know little about him, other than that he was a salesman for Marshall Field & Co.   c75

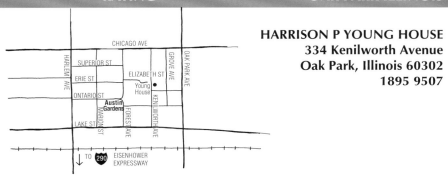

HARRISON P YOUNG HOUSE
334 Kenilworth Avenue
Oak Park, Illinois 60302
1895 9507

Directions: The Young House is on the east side of Kenilworth in the first block south of Chicago Avenue. It can be seen to the east of the Laura Gale House (p71), although there is no direct route through Elizabeth Court.

Accessibility: The front of the house can be seen from the street.

■ This house was built in the 1870s by William E Coman and was remodeled by the later owner, Mr Young (AS). Young was a purchasing agent. Its steeply pitched roof makes it untypical of other Wright houses in this neighborhood, though it is characteristic of his work of the 1890s. It is quite similar to the Wright remodeling for AW Hebert (p40). The decade preceding the turn of the century was a period of great development and experimentation for Wright, which evolved into the Prairie period.   c96

OSCAR B BALCH HOUSE
611 North Kenilworth Avenue
Oak Park, Illinois 60302
1911 1102

Directions: North across Chicago Avenue and beyond the schoolyard is the continuation of Kenilworth Avenue. The house is one block north of Chicago Avenue. One must drive north of Chicago Avenue on Grove Avenue, for one block to Iowa Street and back west to Kenilworth. The house is on the west side of the street.

Accessibility: The house can be seen from the street.

■ The plan with its first-floor living rooms and three-part space is similar to that of the Cheney House (p84) and the Coonley House, but on a smaller scale (p91). It was one of the first designs executed after Wright's return from Europe with Mamah Cheney. The varnished wood and grey stucco contribute to the ungainly effect of the design.

In 1907, Balch and his partner, Frank Pebbles, built a Wright-designed shop on Lake Street in downtown Oak Park (p74).   c76

(Across the street is the house that Ernest Hemingway's mother designed with the architect Henry G Fiddelke. Hemingway lived here from the age of six to eighteen.)

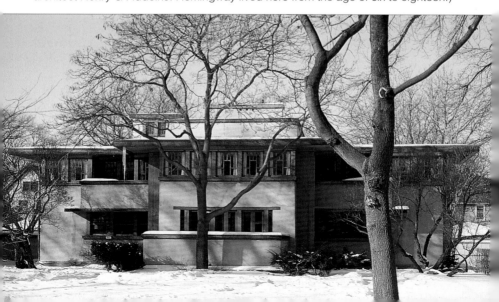

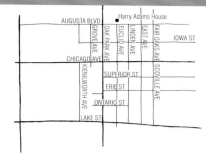

Directions: The house is a block east of Oak Park Avenue and two blocks north of Chicago Avenue.

Accessibility: The main façade of the house can be seen from the street.

■ This is the last of Wright's designs for Oak Park and the second design to be completed after his European sojourn. The art glass in the front door is of particular note. The base glass is the typical straw amber with an iridescent spray fired onto it. As one moves past the door the light reflections sparkle because each small piece of glass is set at a different angle within the metal came. This house was under construction at the same time as Midway Gardens (p126). It is very important to locate the Adams family and find out if there was any Wright-designed furniture for this house.

Try watching the art glass in the front door and observe the changes in it as you walk or drive from one side to the other.   c72

Furter east on the north side of Augusta Boulevard is a house where Edgar Rice Burrows, the author of the Tarzan, the Apeman, series, lived.

WILLIAM E MARTIN HOUSE
636 North East Avenue
Oak Park, Illinois 60302
1902 0304

Directions: East Avenue is three blocks east of Oak Park Avenue and nearly bisects the Village of Oak Park. The house is two blocks north of Chicago Avenue on the east side of the street.

Accessibility: The house can be seen from the street.

■ William was the brother of Darwin D Martin of Buffalo (see East volume) and was his partner in Martin & Martin, manufacturers of stove and shoe polish. Martin patented a method of printing on tin cans and designed a primitive system for traffic controls. He drove a Stanley Steamer. He also awarded the E-Z Polish commission to Wright (p117).

The house has one of the greatest interiors of the Prairie era. The trim contains the entire first floor and a second strip defines each separate space. The decks add to the definition. Standing in the reception hall one is immediately oriented to the entire floor without entering any of the rooms. The third floor is scaled for the children who use it as their playroom. This area includes two adjustable chairs built-in at the doors to the small porch. There was a full compliment of furniture for the house, which has nearly all surfaced in the auction houses.   c73

HARRY C GOODRICH HOUSE
534 North East Avenue
Oak Park, Illinois 60302
1896 9601

Directions: This house is one block north of Chicago Avenue on the east side of East Avenue.

Accessibility: The house can be seen from the street.

■ Goodrich designed attachments for sewing machines and invented many other useful items. This house, like the Young House (p79), is another design dating from Wright's learning decade leading up to 1900. Take particular note of how Wright took the base of the house up and over the basement window on the south façade.   c77

EDWIN H CHENEY HOUSE
520 North East Avenue
Oak Park, Illinois 60302
1904 0401

Map showing street grid with AUGUSTA BLVD, CHICAGO AVE, SUPERIOR ST, ERIE ST, ONTARIO ST, LAKE ST running horizontally and GROVE AVE, OAK PARK AVE, EUCLID AVE, LINDEN AVE, EAST AVE, FAIR OAKS AVE, SCOVILLE AVE, KENILWORTH AVE, IOWA ST, with Cheney House marked.

Directions: The Cheney House is on East Avenue in the first block north of Chicago Avenue on the east side of the street.

Accessibility: The house can be seen from the street and is now operating as a bed and breakfast.

■ The house has a great interior design, the three front rooms are defined by low decks that also hold the front wall from being pushed out by the weight of the roof. There is an opening in the chimney that lets light into the back bedroom hallway. The Cheneys lived on Lake Street in Oak Park before the house was built. Edwin's wife, Mamah, had a sister, Lizzie, who moved here with the family when the house was completed, presumably as a nanny. She also taught in Oak Park.

In 1909, Mamah Cheney left her family to go to Europe with Wright. She was tragically murdered at Taliesin along with her two children in 1914. Mr Cheney remarried in Detroit and lived in the house until 1926 when he moved to a Georgian-style house in St Louis. There he worked for the Wagner Electric Company. c75

WILLIAM G FRICKE HOUSE
540 Fair Oaks Avenue
Oak Park, Illinois 60302
1901 0201

Directions: The house is on the southeast corner of Iowa Street and Fair Oaks Avenue, one block north of Chicago Avenue. Fair Oaks Avenue is in the same line as Scoville Avenue but changes its name at Chicago Avenue.

Accessibility: The two major façades can be seen from the street.

■ In 1900, Fricke was secretary of the CF Weber Co. He, however, died after living in the house for only five years. The house's drawings are dated 9 December 1901. Emma Martin (not related to William or Darwin, see p82 and East volume, respectively) bought the house in 1907 and requested some alterations from Wright. It is a very tall house for a Prairie design. There is a strong oriental feel to the frame at the entry.   c75

(Across Iowa Avenue is a Lawrence Buck design and east across the alley from it is another example of the *Ladie's Home Journal* 'Fireproof House' of April 1907 for $5,000, as rendered by Wright's former draftsman John Van Bergen.)

ROLLIN FURBECK HOUSE
515 Fair Oaks Avenue
Oak Park, Illinois 60302
1897 9801

Directions: The house is on the west side of Fair Oaks Avenue, a few houses north of Chicago Avenue.

Accessibility: The house can be seen from the street.

■ 'This first emphatically forward-looking design excites with its remarkable experimentation. The towering central pavilion makes it even taller on an elevated site. The very open "picture window" on the first floor contrasts sharply with the recessed diamond-paned windows above.' (AS)

The house was a wedding present from Warren Furbeck, Rollin's father. Rollin apparently did not enjoy the house as much as was expected. He moved after only a year to a house designed for him by George Washington Maher on Home Avenue, and later moved to New York to work as a stockbroker. This house was designed six months after that for his brother, George (p88).   c76

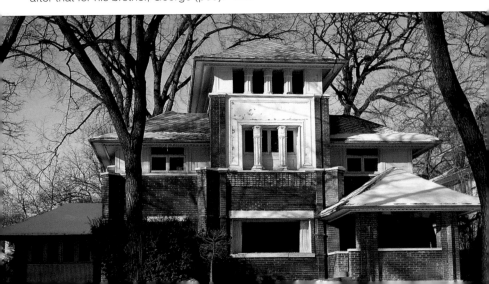

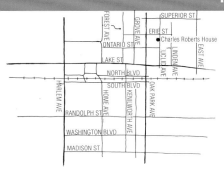

CHARLES E ROBERTS HOUSE
321 North Euclid Avenue
Oak Park, Illinois 60302
1896 9603

Directions: One block east of Oak Park Avenue is Euclid Avenue. The Roberts House is two blocks south of Chicago Avenue and three blocks north of Lake Street on the west side of the street.

Accessibility: The house and stable can be seen from the street.

■ Born in 1843, Roberts lived until 1934. He was on the Unity Temple building committee and recommended Wright as the designer for the new church. As the owner of the Chicago Screw Company factory, he commissioned some unexecuted designs from Wright (Opus #9704). A mechanic, he also invented the Roberts's electric car. His daughter, Isabel, became Wright's secretary and occupied a house paid for by her mother Mary (p55). Mrs Roberts was the sister of Warren Hickox, of Kankakee (East volume). The Roberts's son, Chapin, attended Hillside Home School (UGL volume).

In 1896, the original 1879 Burnham & Root house was remodeled by Wright. The stable, which is now a separate property, may also have been altered by him. In 1929, the stable was reworked and moved by Roberts's son-in-law, Charles E White.   c95

GEORGE FURBECK HOUSE
223 North Euclid Avenue
Oak Park, Illinois 60302
1897 9701

Directions: The house is two blocks north of Lake Street on Euclid Avenue, which is one block east of Oak Park Avenue. The house is on the east side of the street.

Accessibility: The house can be seen from the street.

■ Like the other Furbeck House (p86), this was a wedding present from the father, investor Warren Furbeck. George was the first of five sons. He lived in the house for only two years before moving. The large dormers on the second floor were added much later. The porch was enclosed in 1922. These alterations make the house appear much more awkward than the original design.   c76

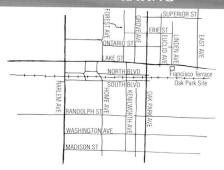

FRANCISCO TERRACE SITE
(formerly Chicago, now in Oak Park)
Lake Street at Linden Avenue
Oak Park, Illinois 60302
1895 9502

Directions: This buiding is on Lake Street, two blocks east of Oak Park Avenue on the south side of the street.

Accessibility: The building can be seen from the street.

■ One of the first and the best of the Prairie School revival projects. In 1973, this apartment block in Chicago, commissioned by Edward C Waller (see p118), was demolished. Realtor John Baird, historian Devereaux Bowly and architect Ben Weese (brother of architect Harry Weese) salvaged the terra cotta ornament and, in 1978, installed it in this building (AS). The overall dimensions of this adaptation are much smaller than the original but its height is about the same. This is a much better use of the decorative fragments of a demolished building than Sullivan's arch from his Chicago Stock Exchange Building, now on display in a garden on the east side of the Art Institute on Columbus Drive in downtown Chicago.   c96

FERDANAND F TOMEK HOUSE
150 Nuttail Road
Riverside, Illinois 60546
1907 0711

GPS: N 41 49.916
       W 87 49.031

Coonley Kindergarten
Teachers' Residence by
Drummond

Directions: Riverside is south of Oak Park just west of Harlem Avenue. The streets of Riverside were laid out by Frederick Law Olmstead, the designer of New York's Central Park, and Calvert Vaux in 1869 as a garden suburb. Take Longcommon from Harlem about 1.5 miles as it curves around and intersects Bartram. Nuttail is parallel to Longcommon and the house is across the parkway from it to the north.

Accessibility: The house can be seen from the street.

■ The Tomek House was a rough draft for the Robie House (p125), although this was not a conscious decision on Wright's part. It was only later that he refined the Tomek House and it became the Robie House for another client. This is one of the few Wright designs that has a door on the face of the building, giving it a direct entry. An earlier house with this feature that comes to mind is the Winslow House (p52).   c80

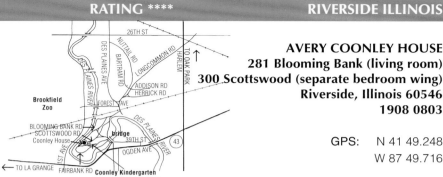

AVERY COONLEY HOUSE
281 Blooming Bank (living room)
300 Scottswood (separate bedroom wing)
Riverside, Illinois 60546
1908 0803

GPS: N 41 49.248
W 87 49.716

Directions: From the Tomek House (p90) continue southwest on Longcommon and across the railroad tracks. Keep to the right, the house is four blocks down on the right.

Accessibility: The dining room side of the house can be seen from the street..

■ Coonley graduated with the Harvard Class of 1894. In 1901 he married Queene Ferry of the Ferry Seed Company of Detroit, the same year his brother, Howard, married Leslie May of Boston. Howard also lived in Riverside and oversaw the Coonley Manufacturing Co in Clyde, Illinois. Avery began in business working for the National Malleable Castings Co. A third brother, John Stuart, lived on East End Avenue near the Robie House and shared an office with Avery in the McCormick Building in downtown Chicago. John Stuart and Avery were Christian Scientists while Howard was Episcopalian. Avery Coonley was a director of *The Dial,* a magazine owned by the Brownes of Brownes's Bookstore (p134).

The Coonleys only lived in the house for about eight years. The property extended over the entire end of the peninsula. The main rooms of the house are on the second level, in much the same manner as the Thomas House (p73). This is one of the first

examples of the zoned house. It has three main components: living-room wing, bedroom wing, and kitchen/servants' wing. This idea was expanded upon in the Johnson House some thirty years later and became Wingspread (UGL Volume). The Coonleys did their homework before commissioning the architect by seeing most of Wright's other work and interviewing him at his studio

The design of the house was dictated by the tenets of the Christian Science Church, which requires that its practitioners conduct interviews. There were two stairways so the interviewees could not see each other when entering or leaving.

As part of the estate, Wright designed a stable at 336 Coonley Road and a gardener's cottage to the east of the stables at 290 Scottswood. Jens Jensen landscaped the property.

The house was fully furnished. There was a full set of furniture for all the rooms except for the dining room, which encompassed all of the fabrics including the curtains and the rugs. The drawings and yarn samples can be seen in the Prairie Archives at the Milwaukee Art Museum as a part of the Niedecken-Wallbridge Collection.

The property was subdivided in the 1950s. The main building was divided between the bedroom wing and the living room. The other buildings were sold as separate properties and were converted into living quarters.

In 1900, Coonley commissioned a school from Wright for Crosbyton, Texas (Opus # 0012). Crosbyton was the site of the Coonley Bassett Livestock Company and the Crosbyton Co, a merchandising and manufacturing company. The company nearly went bankrupt but was saved by selling its railroad spur to the Santa Fe line. William Drummond designed a town plan of Crosbyton, Texas, for Coonley some time later but it appears to be unexecuted. c78

COONLEY PLAYHOUSE
350 Fairbanks Road
Riverside, Illinois 60546
1912 1201

GPS: N 41 49.168
         W 87 49.707

Directions: The kindergarten is one block south of the main teachers' residence on Fairbanks Road and faces the park that borders this end of the peninsula.

Accessibility: The building can be seen from the street.

■ The Coonleys, who felt very strongly about education, asked Wright to design this kindergarten for their daughter and other neighborhood children.

The school has since been converted into a residence. The art-glass windows now in place are new reproductions copied from the originals which were removed in the 1950s and 60s. To tone down the effect, the white side of the glass was intended to be exposed to the exterior instead of the primary colors.

Coonley also commissioned William Drummond to produce another school building, it has often been confused with Wright's design. c77

(In nearby Brookfield, a Wright-designed house for MB Hilly is reported to have been built and later demolished. There is no evidence, however, that it was ever constructed. If anyone has any information about the house or Mr Hilly, please come forward.)

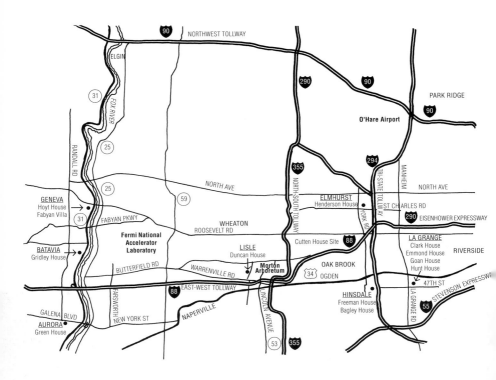

■ These cities and towns grew up for many of the same reasons as did those of the north shore (p16), easy rail and road links. There was, however, more farming in this area than on the north shore. An interesting trend is clear in these examples. Most of Wright's buildings occur in groups. Those along the Fox River would constitute one group, Hinsdale and La Grange two additional groups. No research has been done into this phenomenon so far.

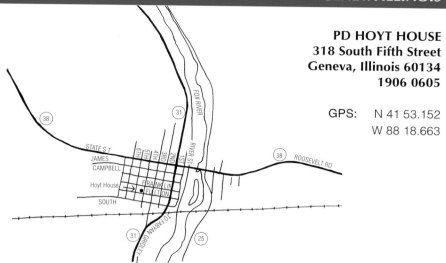

PD HOYT HOUSE
318 South Fifth Street
Geneva, Illinois 60134
1906 0605

GPS: N 41 53.152
           W 88 18.663

Directions: Geneva is on the west bank of the Fox River. The house is four blocks south of State Street on the west side of 5th Street.

Accessibility: The house is partly hidden behind a tall wall along the sidewalk.

■ Hoyt was a pharmacist who was instrumental in bringing the Gridley work (p97) to Wright. There is an unusual central front entry. A tall wall was added in the 1980s along the front sidewalk. The House was built by contractors August and Oscar Wilson of Geneva. The muntin patterns of the windows spell out the initial 'H' for Hoyt.   c78

GEORGE FABYAN VILLA
1511 Batavia Road
Geneva, Illinois 60134
1907 0703

GPS: N 41 52.181
W 88 18.767

Directions: The house is in the park just off South Batavia Road, Illinois Route 31, about half a mile north of Fabyan Parkway.

Accessibility: The villa can be seen from the street, but one must park in the parking lot accessed south of the villa just a few feet north of Fabyan Parkway.

■ George Fabyan was born in Boston in 1867 into a wealthy family, which founded a George Fabyan Chair at Harvard Medical School. His father's company, Bliss, Fabyan & Co, dealt in cotton textiles. In 1903, he came to Chicago as a representative of the company. He was involved in many areas, including acoustics, cryptology and horticulture. He died at home on 17 May 1936 at the age of sixty-nine.

In 1905, Fabyan bought 5 acres and the house on the Joel D Harvey farm. He held over 600 acres. Wright's remodeling of the house consumed the earlier building. Fabyan favored suspended furniture, hung from chains or rope.   c96

(In 1907, Wright built the Fox River Country Club on the Fabyan estate southwest of the villa. This was an addition to an earlier building. It burned down in about 1910.)

AW GRIDLEY HOUSE
605 North Batavia Road
Batavia, Illinois 60510
1906 0604

GPS: N 41 51.733
W 88 18.803

Directions: Further south of the Fabyan Villa and on the west side of Illinois Route 31, just north of Timber Trail, is the Gridley House.

Accessibility: Though set back from the road, the house can be seen from the street.

■ Although more block-like and less elegant than the Ingalls House (p56), the first-floor plan is nearly identical in its disposition of rooms. Gridley did not live in the house very long. He met Wright through Hoyt, and Hoyt went on to introduce him to Fabyan. During the summer, breezes sweep across the open porches. These suggest that Wright had some knowledge of aerodynamics as the overhangs, the porch wall and the pitched roof create an airfoil; the air is forced to increase in speed as it crosses the porch. c74

WILLIAM B GREENE HOUSE
**1300 West Garfield Avenue
Aurora, Illinois 60506
1912 1203**

GPS: N 41 45.605
      W 88 20.805

Directions: Aurora is west of the Fox River, south of Interstate 88. The house is on the west side of town on a beautiful street. Take Galena Boulevard west to Gladstone and then south two blocks to Garfield.

Accessibility: The house can be seen from the street.

■ Greene was born in Lisle, Illinois, in 1886 and graduated from the University of Illinois-Urbana in 1908 in mechanical engineering. In 1916 he formed a partnership, the Barber-Greene Company, which was the world's largest manufacturer of asphalt-paving machines. Both the plan and the details of the house are so awkward it has been suggested that it was not designed by Wright but by the client's college roommate, Harry Robinson, who was responsible for the organization of the entire project through Wright's office. Robinson supervised the construction and the later additions to the house. It is in good condition but the original furniture has been sold at auction in recent years.   c74

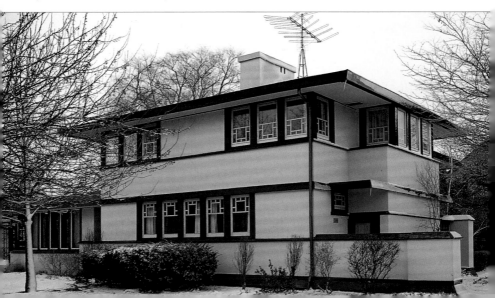

DON DUNCAN HOUSE
(Erdman Prefab #1)
2255 Edgebrooke
Lisle, Illinois 60532
1957 5518

GPS: N 41 48.950

        W 88 06.016

Directions: Exit Interstate 88 at interchange 146 at Illinois Route 53, the Morton Arboretum, and drive south to the first west road, Warrenville Road, a few hundred feet south of the Interstate. Drive west on Warrenville Road back under the Interstate, past Yackley Avenue, to Leask Lane and turn north. Leask is the western border of the Arboretum. Continue north for 0.9 miles and then east on Edgebrooke Road for 0.25 miles. The house is on the southwest corner.

Accessibility: The house can be seen from the street.

■ This is another example of a person acquiring a Wright-designed house without having directly approached Wright and commissioned a custom-built house from him. The Duncans saw the 1956 *House & Home* article that featured the Erdman Prefabs and contacted Erdman for one of them. The original cost of the house was $47,000, an expensive house at the time. The Duncans did eventually meet Wright on a trip to Taliesin West. Duncan was a University of Illinois graduate in electrical engineering and worked for the Western Electric Co.   c96

WARREN H FREEMAN HOUSE
103 North Washington Street
Hinsdale, Illinois 60521
1903 0312

GPS: N 41 48.283
         W 87 55.748

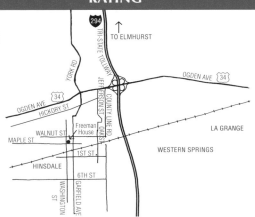

Directions: Exit Interstate 294 westbound US Highway 34, Ogden Avenue, and continue on for three-quarters of a mile to York Road and turn south. Drive south for 0.6 miles past the curve where York becomes Garfield. Continue south to Maple and turn west one block to Washington. The house is on the northeast corner across from the library.

Accessibility: Though screened by various bushes and trees, the house can be seen from the street.

■ This was a rental property belonging to Freeman, a Unitarian, who lived nearby. As HR Hitchcock has pointed out *In the Nature of Materials* (1942) the house was altered in execution. Though the plan is nearly identical to the published plan, the exterior details, such as the art glass windows, are not typical Wright. The existing art glass was installed by the current owners after they purchased several panels at auction.   c96

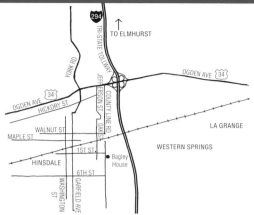

FREDERICK BAGLEY HOUSE
121 South County Line Road
Hinsdale, Illinois 60521
1894 9401

GPS: N 41 48.083
      W 87 55.050

Directions: Exit Interstate 294 at US Highway 34, Ogden Avenue, and drive west to the intersection at Jefferson Street and south to Hickory, then west to Oak. Turn south and continue for 0.8 miles to Walnut, take it further south over the one lane wooden bridge over the railroad tracks and then back east to County Line Road. The house is two blocks south on the east side of the street.

Accessibility: The house can be seen from the street.

■ Frederick Bagley was a marble importer who only lived in the house for three years. He may have been a relative of JJ Bagley who built a house in Grand Beach, Michigan, about twenty years later, Opus #1601 (see UGL volume); no documents have been found that establish this one way or the other. In 1894, Wright produced some designs for Frederick Bagley's business, including a communion rail and altar sculpture. c76

FB HENDERSON HOUSE
301 South Kenilworth Avenue
Elmhurst, Illinois 60126
1901 0104

GPS: N 41 53.516
      W 87 56.633

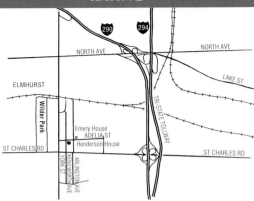

Directions: Elmhurst is at the far west end of Interstate 290. Exit at interchange 14 at St Charles Road and drive west for a mile to Kenilworth Avenue then turn north, one block east of York Road. The house is on the southeast corner of Adelia Street.

Accessibility: The house can be seen from the street.

■ Like the Hickox and Cheney Houses (East volume and p84 of this volume), the house is set high on smooth stucco walls. Recently an owner did a great deal of work to the house. c76

  (Across the street is Walter Burley Griffin's first house, the Emery House, built while he was employed at Wright's studio in 1901. The Wilder Stables, nearby, demolished in 1941, were also probably designed by Griffin, perhaps while he was still working in Wright's office. Wilder's daughter was Mrs Emery. Wilder lived in Oak Park before moving out west to Elmhurst.)

W IRVING CLARK HOUSE
211 South La Grange Road
La Grange, Illinois 60525
1893 9209

GPS: N 41 48.583
            W 87 52.136

Directions: La Grange is east of Hinsdale across Interstate 294, the Tri-State Tollway. Exit the Interstate eastbound at mile 28, Ogden Avenue, US Highway 34, and drive along for 2.3 miles to La Grange Road, US 12/20 and 45, south for half a mile to the house which is on the east side of the street, just south of Elm Avenue.

Accessibility: The house can be seen from the street.

■ This house was originally published as the work of E Hill Turnock, however, an article by Wayne Michael Charney in the May 1978 *Frank Lloyd Wright Newsletter* provided the detailed research that attributed it to Wright; the drawings were originally found by Bruce Pfeiffer at Taliesin. This is the earliest of the La Grange houses.   c95

(The Arthur E Cutten House, Opus #1115, at Downers Grove, northwest of La Grange, was partly constructed in 1911 in accordance with Wright's plans, but was apparently completed by another architect in more of the English-cottage style. The property has been taken over by the County Forest Preserve District and the house has been demolished.)

ROBERT G EMMOND HOUSE
109 South Eighth Avenue
La Grange, Illinois 60525
1892 9202

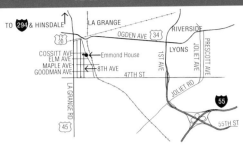

GPS: N 41 48.717
      W 87 51.901

Directions: La Grange is east of Hinsdale across Interstate 294, the Tri-State Tollway. Exit the Interstate at mile 28, Ogden Avenue, US Highway 34, and drive for 2.3 miles to La Grange Road, US 12/20 and 45, then south for half a mile before turning off at Cossitt Avenue north of Elm Avenue. The house is three blocks down on Cossitt on the east side of 8th Avenue.

Accessibility: The house can be seen from the street.

■ Emmond was the roommate of Orrin Goan (see p105) when they both lived on Washington Street in Chicago. The south porch with arched windows was an addition at the time when brick was added to the first floor. The plan is like those of the Gale and Parker Houses in Oak Park (pp61 and 62).   c76

PETER GOAN HOUSE
108 South Eighth Avenue
La Grange, Illinois 60525
1893 9403

GPS: N41 48.716
            W 87 51.916

Directions: La Grange is east of Hinsdale across Interstate 294, the Tri-State Tollway. Exit the Interstate eastbound at mile 28, Ogden Avenue, US Highway 34, and drive for 2.3 miles to La Grange Road, US 12/20 and 45, then south for half a mile to Cossitt Avenue and turn east three blocks to 8th Avenue. The house is south on the west side of the street.

Accessibility: The house can be seen from the street.

■ The house had a large porch as can be seen from a photo in William A Storrer's *Frank Lloyd Wright Companion.* Peter Goan's son was Orrin S Goan, a National Biscuit Company (Nabisco) executive.   c76

    (A set of drawings for the Henry N Cooper House, also intended for La Grange, appear to be part of the portfolio that Wright claimed to have presented to Louis Sullivan before being hired by him. Henry Noble Cooper was born on 2 May 1861 in Salem, Illinois, to John E and Helen E, née Noble, Cooper and had four children. He worked for the Elk Rapids Iron Co, Michigan, before becoming a lawyer after attending the Union College of Law in 1885. He was a real-estate dealer and a vice-president of Fitzsimmons & Connell, public works contractors. He lived in La Grange from before 1905 until about 1917, then moved to 737 Bittersweet, Chicago, just south of the Husser House, p114.)

STEPHEN MB HUNT HOUSE
345 South Seventh Avenue
La Grange, Illinois 60525
1907 0705

GPS: N 41 48.316
     W 87 51.952

Directions: La Grange is east of Hinsdale across Interstate 294, the Tri-State Tollway. Exit the Interstate eastbound at mile 28, Ogden Avenue, US Highway 34, and drive for 2.3 miles to La Grange Road, US 12/20 and 45, south for 0.8 miles to Goodman Avenue. Turn east for two blocks to 7th Avenue and turn south. The house is on the northeast corner of 47th Street and 7th Avenue.

Accessibility: The house can be seen from the street.

■ This is the realization of a proposal made in the April 1907 edition of the *Ladies Home Journal.* It is one of the most economical plans ever devised. By visually borrowing space from other rooms, each room appears much larger than its actual dimensions. It is very economical to build even based on today's dimensional lumber. All of the windows are the same size adding to the economy. Walter Burley Griffin was in Wright's office at this time and executed many exterior variations on this plan. By adding porches to different sides, the house can appear very different as can be seen in the Ravine Bluffs houses (p25). The feature that makes this house a cut above what one might expect is the windows. In the living room the glass extends up to the plane of the ceiling. At the ends of the four large front windows are slit lights that allow the jambs to be free of the wall. c76

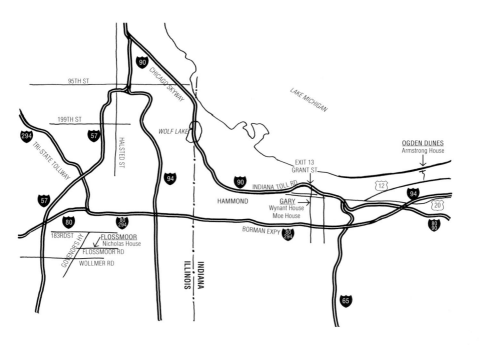

■ As a group, these are the most modest of buildings. Represented here are also the newest discoveries: two Wright designs, discovered in Gary, Indiana, in early 1996 by Chris Meyers. There are, however, more to find, everyone is sure. When visiting Gary, Indiana, please be careful. It has one of the highest rates for violent crime in the US.

FREDERICK D NICHOLAS HOUSE
1136 Brassie Avenue
Flossmoor, Illinois 60422
1906 0607

GPS: N 41 32.474
     W 87 40.624

Directions: Exit Interstate 57 at Vollmer Road eastbound to Govenor's Highway. Turn northeast for a mile to Flossmoor Road and turn east for a mile to Brassie Avenue, and turn south. The house is on the west side of the street just north of Hawthorne Lane, in the block south of Flossmoor Road.

Accessibility: The house can be seen from the street.

■ It is unlikely that Nicholas was one of the Nicholases who promoted the Como Orchards project of Montana or who were associated with the University of Chicago. There was a FD Nichols noted but very little is known about Mr Nicholas. His wife was Mary H Nicholas, whose parents were Mary King and Tappan Halsey. The land was purchased in October 1906 and Nicholas borrowed $4,217 from his father-in-law, presumably to build the house. The land cost $1,200. The original design was a typical four-square plan based, again, on that in the *Ladies Home Journal*, but executed with horizontal wood-board and batten siding. The house was extended and repainted in 1993.   c96

(Flossmoor is near the Indiana State line and the Interstate 90, the Chicago Skyway, which passes through the middle of Wolf Lake. It was the site of a large project designed for Warren McArthur, p122, in the 1890s, Wolf Lake Amusement Park, Opus #9510.)

WILBER WYNANT HOUSE
(American Systems House D-101)
600 Filmore Street
Gary, Indiana 46402
1915-16 1506

GPS: N 41 36.103
        W 87 21.063

Directions: Exit Interstate 90 at Indiana mile 13, Grant Street. Drive south and four blocks down Bucanan Street to 7th Street and then east to Polk Street, back north one block and west to the southwest corner of 6th and Filmore.

Accessibility: The house can be seen from the street.

■ In 1996, this house was identified by Chris Meyers, a former student at the Art Institute of Chicago. It is the model D-101 of the American Systems series, which was first occupied by Wilber Wynant. Although its condition is deteriorating, its fate still remains in question. The discovery of the Wynant House, however, points out that we still do not have a conclusive knowledge of Wright's entire output. There is very little documentation on the majority of the buildings especially from the earliest periods.   c96

INGWALD MOE HOUSE
669 Van Buren Street
Gary, Indiana 46402
1908 0531

GPS: N 41 36.015
W 87 20.468

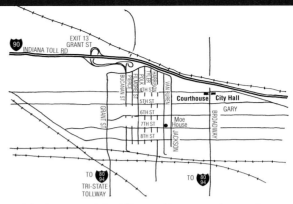

Directions: The house is three blocks east of the Wynant House on the northeast corner of 7th and Van Buren.

Accessibility: The house can be seen from the street.

■ The Moe House has just recently been rediscovered by Chris Meyers. He has located early photographs and the author identified a color rendering by Marion Mahoney, which recently surfaced through Christie's auction house. It certainly owes the large part of its design to the well-known Brown House (p39), though it has several distinctive details. For instance, the Brown House is horizontal board and batten siding, whereas this house is stucco. Moe was a contractor with offices on Washington Street in Chicago, before moving to Gary. A letter discovered by Meyers noted that the house was among the group that came under the joint responsibility of Wright and Herman von Holst when Wright left for Europe and turned over his work to Von Holst.   c96

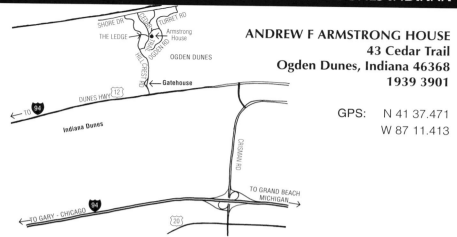

ANDREW F ARMSTRONG HOUSE
43 Cedar Trail
Ogden Dunes, Indiana 46368
1939 3901

GPS: N 41 37.471
W 87 11.413

Directions: Exit Interstate 90 at mile 17, US Highway 12, and drive east for 6 miles along the Dunes Highway to Hillcrest Road. Turn north for 1.5 miles to Ogden Road, then east one short block to Cedar Trail and one more block to the house at the intersection of The Ledge and Cedar Trail. The house is on the east or lake side of the street.

Accessibility: The back of the house can be seen from the street.

■ This is the first Wright design to be constructed anywhere near the Chicago area after the mid-1920s. The house feels more like the Californian Hanna and Bazett Houses with its obtuse angles and finger-jointed brick corners. The original construction was modest, it was only later expanded by Jack Howe.   c95

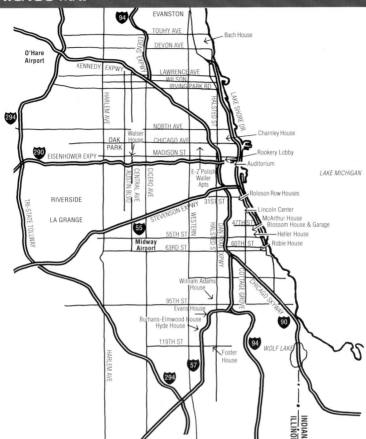

■ Chicago grew at a very rapid rate doubling in population every ten years between 1840 and 1920. As Carl Sandberg's 'City of Big Shoulders,' the people were never shy about new ideas and approaches. This attitude led to more successes than failures. It also led people to seek unusual solutions to everyday problems like housing. Not all of Wright's experiments were well received. There are more lessons to be learned in these buildings than most can imagine. Chicago grew by absorbing other cities and towns such as Lake View, Hyde Park and Kenwood. In 1901 Daniel Burnham reorganized all of these into an urban whole and gave it a powerful grid system. He simplified it, taking the fourteen or so Lake Streets and renaming them. A telephone book sized guide to new and old names and numbers is still used. The zero-zero point of the grid system is at State and Madison, at Sullivan's Carson, Pirie, Scott Building. Everything can be found from that point. There are eight blocks to the mile in this system.

CHICAGO-NORTH SITES

See map above and on p115 for locations.

OSCAR STEFFENS HOUSE SITE, 7631 North Sheridan Road, Chicago 60626
1909 0909

■ The Steffens House was built just off the shore of Lake Michigan, though not facing it. This large house was converted into a restaurant during the early 1930s. It was known as the King's Arms until its demolition in April 1963. Some of the art glass windows were salvaged from the building and installed in the Arkansas vacation home of a Chicago architect. The house was another variation on the Isabel Roberts House scheme (p55). The art glass is noteworthy because it is one of the very few to use blue glass. More abstract than most others of the period, it precedes that of the Little House of 1913 (see UGL volume). Steffens worked for the First National Bank of Chicago. He lived in the house only a short time before selling it to Otto Bach, the brother of Emil Bach (p115). An undistinguished yellow brick apartment now occupies the site.

LK HORNER HOUSE SITE, 1331 Sherwin Avenue
1908 0807

■ This house, which is now demolished, is a near duplicate of several others including the Walser House (p116), the Barton and the De Rhodes Houses (East volume). The central portion of the house was a single room broken into three spaces in the same manner as the Cheney and Henderson Houses (pp84 and 102), using low decks to differentiate the spaces. Samuel Horner was the president of the Horner Piano Company. In 1918, he died and his wife moved to Evanston. Though in photographs the house often appears to have a flat roof like the Laura Gale House (p71), it actually had a hipped roof with wide eaves.

CATHERINE WRIGHT GRAVE SITE, Section 105T, Rosehill Cemetery, 5800 North Ravenswood (and 5800 Western)

The cemetery is open nearly every day from 8.30am to 4.00pm. Phone 733/561-5940.

■ Wright's first wife, Catherine Tobin Wright (1871-1959), is buried here with her parents, Samuel and Flora, and grandfather, Moses. The graves have red-granite headstones.

JOSEPH J HUSSER HOUSE SITE, 730 (was 180) Buena Avenue 1899 9901

■ An official in the Christian Science Church, Husser was an executive for John M Williams, a real-estate broker. He bought this lot from James B Waller. After Lake Shore Drive was extended, it was a good distance from the shore and buildings were built up around it. According to a building permit, an apartment block was erected here in 1923.

WILLIAM MᴀᴄHARG HOUSE SITE, 4632 Beacon Avenue 1891 9002

■ Now demolished, this house was an official Adler & Sullivan project and not an independent Wright commission. The project was initiated in the Adler & Sullivan offices by the client Dr CH Berry. When in 1902 Berry died, MacHarg, who lived in the house with Berry, purchased it from his widow. A plumbing contractor for Adler & Sullivan, MacHarg was later associated with Wright through the Luxfer Prism Company. Before moving to this house, Berry lived on the near-west side and MacHarg lived on the near-north side of the Loop. They may have been related through marriage, but this has never been confirmed. Berry and Macharg would have used the Wilson 'L' (see below).

STOHR ARCADE SITE, Wilson 'L' Stop at Wilson Avenue 1909 0910

■ For such a large building it had a very short life (built 1909 and demolished December 1922). This is unfortunate as usually structures around the elevated stations remain unchanged for an extremely long time. Most stations are nearly original on the north line. The second-floor arched windows had a reverse arch to the triple muntins that gave them an oriental look. The building that replaced it accommodated the Chicago Transit 'L' line and the North Shore interurban line. Peter C Stohr was a Union Pacific Railroad official.

SULLIVAN GRAVE SITE, Graceland Cemetery 4001 North Clark Street at Irving Park Road

Graceland Cemetery is open from 8.30am to 4.00pm. Phone 733/525-1105.

■ Louis Sullivan's last years were tragic. Though without an income, he could still draw with a flourish. This is evident in his last executed design for the Krause Music Store at 4600 Lincoln Avenue. George Grant Elmslie designed this gravestone and, presumably, burned Sullivan's papers. Adler & Sullivan's Getty Tomb is at the north end of the cemetery.

(Wright designed a house for Mrs Aline Devin in 1896 for Chicago, Opus #9603, and another ten years later for Eliot, Maine, Opus #0613.)

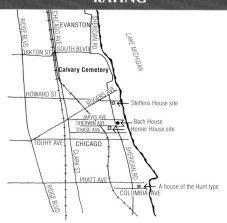

EMIL BACH HOUSE
7415 North Sheridan Road
Chicago 60626
1915 1501

GPS: N 42 01.000
        W 87 39.935

Directions: The house is on the east side of Sheridan Road, just a few blocks south of Evanston and two blocks north of Touhy Avenue.

Accessibility: The house can be seen from the street.

■ This is Wright's last small urban commission. It came from Emil Bach, a foreman of the Bach Brick Company. The plan is a variation of the 1905 *Ladies Home Journal* 'Fireproof House' for $5,000. It has the most elaborate entrance path of any small house, only rivaled by the Cheney House (p84). With its deep-set windows and projecting trellises, the house can clearly be dated after the Prairie era. The house is lucky that it retains the lot to the south. Unfortunately, it has not been lived in for nearly twenty years. There is now a gate and a chain-link fence across the front of the property.   c80

JJ WALSER HOUSE
42 North Central Avenue
Chicago 60644
1903 0306

GPS: N 41 52.853
      W 87 45.909

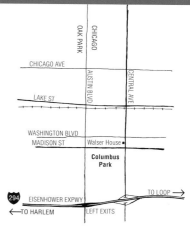

Directions: Central Avenue (5600 west) and Madison (0 north–south) is just a half mile east of Oak Park. The house is squeezed between two apartment buildings and is set back from the front of them.

Accessibility: The house can be seen from the street.

■ This is a near copy of the Barton and De Rhodes Houses (see East volume). The space that runs throughout the central part of the house contains a single room with three different spaces. This definition is accomplished in the same manner as the Cheney House (p84) with trim and low decks. The house has had a difficult life and was not properly maintained for many years. The art glass windows were removed and sold in order to save the building.   c80

E-Z POLISH FACTORY
3005 West Carroll Avenue
Chicago 60612
1905 0504

GPS: N 41 53.252
W 87 42.116

Directions: Exit Interstate 290 at California Avenue and drive north 0.8 miles to Fulton Street, south of the Lake Street 'L' tracks. Turn west for two blocks to Sacramento Boulevard and turn north to Carroll Avenue.

Accessibility: The building can be seen from the street.

■ The factory was built by Martin & Martin Stove Polish Company in a business venture initiated by two brothers, William E and Darwin D Martin. For Wright, the structure was an exercise in concrete-construction techniques. This is one of the least decorative buildings of Wright's career.   c73

(To the east on Caroll Avenue are the buildings that once housed Winslow Brothers Iron Works, see p52 for the Winslow House.)

WALLER APARTMENTS
2840 to 2858 West Walnut Street
Chicago 60612
1895 9504

GPS: N 42 53.135
W 87 41.907

Directions: Exit Interstate 290 at California Avenue (2800 west) and drive north for 0.7 miles to Walnut and turn west to the end of the block. The houses are on the north side of the street.

Accessibility: The apartments can be seen from the street.

■ Originally five units of four apartments were built – one block was destroyed by fire in 1968. The remaining buildings are now being converted into two townhouses with each unit containing two houses. In its detailing, this scheme is much simpler than its neighbor to the north, Francisco Terrace, which was built later. This is one of the smaller projects that was commissioned by real-estate magnate Edward C Waller (see p49).

(Francisco Terrace on 253 North Francisco Avenue, Opus #9502, was built in 1895. It was demolished in 1974 when the salvaged parts of the building were relocated, see p89. Also constructed for Waller, it was known as 'honeymoon terrace' because of its many newly wed tenants. The building had a 175-foot-long courtyard in the center.)

ROBERT W ROLOSON ROW HOUSES
3213 South Calumet Avenue
Chicago 60616
1894 9404

GPS: N 41 50.157
           W 87 37.085

Directions: Exit Interstate 90/94 at mile 54, 31st Street and drive east 0.7 miles to Calumet Avenue. Turn south two blocks where the buildings are on the east side of the street across from Douglas School.

Accessibility: The houses can be seen from the street.

■ This is the only set of Wright row houses ever built. Roloson was the son-in-law of Edward C Waller. A second scheme appears in drawings, but it is not clear if this was a later remodeling of the same building or a rethinking of it while it was under construction. The present interiors are a mere shadow of Wright's well-planned originals.

Robert M Roloson married Waller's daughter in 1894. His father, Robert W Roloson was a member of the Board of Trade and director of the Diamond Match Company.   c95

LINCOLN CENTER (ABRAHAM)
**700 East Oakwood Boulevard
(39th Street)
Chicago 60653
1903 0010**

GPS: N 41 29.355
W 87 36.583

Directions: Exit Interstate 90/94 at 39th Street, Pershing Road, go east for a mile to Langley and turn south one block to Oakwood. Alternatively, from the east, exit Lake Shore Drive at Oakwood and drive west for half a mile. The center is on the northeast corner of Oakwood and Langley.

Accessibility: The center can be seen from the street. The interior is open during business hours.

■ Wright lived in this neighborhood when he first arrived in Chicago from Madison in 1887. Through activities at the 1887 Joseph Lyman Silsbee-designed All Souls' Church (now demolished) across the street, he met his first wife, Catherine Tobin. The Lincoln Center was a project of his Uncle Jenkin Lloyd Jones, which was designed in collaboration with Dwight H Perkins. Both Wright and Perkins dropped out of the project before its completion citing the stubborness of Rev Jones. Between 1971 and 1976, its interior was renovated in line with the university's requirements (AS). c87

CHICAGO-SOUTH SITES
See map on p120.

LOUIS SULLIVAN HOUSE SITE (ALBERT), 4575 Lake Park Avenue
1892 9207

■ The house, which has now been demolished, was built for Sullivan's mother, Adrienne, who was to share her home with Louis, but died before it was completed. Consequently, Louis' brother, Albert, took it over. Albert Sullivan was a vice-president of Illinois Central Railroad. Adler & Sullivan designed several commuter stations at 39th and 43rd Streets in Chicago and the main terminal at New Orleans, now demolished, which Wright and George Grant Elmslie drafted. Both Wright and Elmslie initialed their drawings. The IC railroad line still runs along the lake east of this house. It has been said that Sullivan loved to take walks. It is therefore difficult to understand how Wright expected to conceal his alleged moonlighting from his employer: the three large houses that he is reputed to have designed outside office hours were located within three blocks of Sullivan's home. All of the houses, Harlan, Blossom and McArthur were published under the name of the architect Cecil Corwin. One wonders if these clients weren't friends of either Rev Jones or Wright's father-in-law, Samuel Tobin.

DR ALLISON HARLAN HOUSE SITE, 4414 Greenwood Avenue
1892 9204

■ Dr Harlan was a professor of dental surgery. It is surprising that there are so few photos of the house, and none in color, since it was not lost until 1963, when it was destroyed by fire. According to Tim Samuelson of the Commission of Chicago Landmarks, there is no evidence that Elbert Hubbard, chief salesman of the Larkin Company and founder of the Roycrofters, ever owned this property as was reported by another author.

FRANCIS APARTMENTS SITE, 4304 Forestville Avenue
1895 9501

■ Situated on a commercial street with businesses on the first floor of the north (right) wing, the apartments exhibited good planning. Demolished in 1971, there are, however, no surviving photographs of them. Terra cotta was used on the first-floor walls of the exterior. On the east façade, there was an entry to a small courtyard with elaborate gates that are now at the Art Institute of Chicago. The Francis Apartments were built for the Terra Haute Trust another Edward Waller company (see p118).

SAMUEL C TOBIN HOUSE, 4721 South Kimbark Street

■ This is the site of the home that Samuel C Tobin (1842-1916) and his wife Flora Parish Tobin (1843-1916) built in 1885. The Tobins became members of All Souls' Church after they moved into the house in about 1886. Their daughter Catherine married Frank Lloyd Wright there on 1 June1889, and Rev Jenkin Lloyd Jones presided over the ceremony. The Tobins are buried in adjacent plots at Rosehill Cemetery (p114).

WARREN McARTHUR HOUSE
4852 South Kenwood Avenue
Chicago 60615
1892 9205

GPS: N 41 48.390
W 87 35.605

Directions: Exit South Lake Shore Drive at 47th Street and drive west for a quarter of a mile to Woodlawn, pass three blocks, and turn south. On 48th or 49th Street, continue for two blocks east to Kenwood. The house is on the west side of the street, second from the south corner.

Accessibility: The house can be seen from the street.

■ This design is contemporary with the other gambrel-roof residence, the Bagley House, Hinsdale (p101). The style is similar to that of Cecil Corwin and Joseph Lyman Silsbee. The house was first published as Corwin's, although it was included in an article by Robert C Spencer in 1900 as Wright's work. McArthur's partner in the Ham Lantern Co was EE Boynton (East volume). McArthur's sons were responsible for the Arizona Biltmore Hotel (West volume) and he was a potential manufacturer for the Johnson Wax tubular furniture. In about 1901, several years after the initial construction, Wright completed the interior alterations and the coach house was erected. The details of this additional work are similar to those of the Thomas House (p73).   c75

ABOVE
Garage of the George
Blossom House   c96

GEORGE BLOSSOM HOUSE
4858 South Kenwood Avenue
Chicago 60615
1892 9201

GPS:	N 41 48.357
	W 87 35.627
UTM:	16 T 045 0677
	462 8407

Directions: Exit South Lake Shore Drive at 47th Street and drive west for a quarter of a mile to Woodlawn, pass three blocks, and turn south. On 48th or 49th Street, continue for two blocks east to Kenwood. The house is on the west side of the street, at the south corner.

Accessibility: The house can be seen from the street.

■ This building at first appears to be a traditional colonial house, however, after a closer study the modern innovations that Wright introduced become apparent. It is the interior that departs from the conventional style of the exterior. The living room is at the center of the house with the staircase on the north side and a Palladian window on the south side. After seeing the quality of the design, Daniel Burnham offered Wright the position of chief designer in his large firm which he declined.   c75

The garage dates from 1907 (Opus #0701), see photo on p122. It was built complete with a turntable, grease pits and a chauffeur's quarters upstairs. It was in poor shape for many years and is now a single family residence.

ISADORE HELLER HOUSE
5132 South Woodlawn Avenue
Chicago 60615
1896 9606

GPS: N 41 48.125
W 87 35.875
UTM: 16 T 045 0327
462 7957

Directions: Exit South Lake Shore Drive at 47th Street and drive west 0.4 miles to Woodlawn and south to 51st Street.

Accessibility: The house can be seen from the street.

■ The frieze was modeled by Richard Bock. Two-toned brick was used on the second story. The entry is at the side of the house. Tapestry brick was a technique promoted by Louis Sullivan and used sparingly by Wright. The sizable house was planned with four large bedrooms and a small room for a servant. The third floor was to contain a playroom much like the Martin House in Oak Park (p82). This may be the first use of stiff, colonial cames in Wright's art glass. The stairhall windows may have been manufactured by the new Luxfer Prism Co, using William Herman Winslow's patented technique for setting glass in metal (see pp52-53). There are no photos of the interior while the Hellers were in residence and it is not known if any Wright-designed furniture was made for it. c80

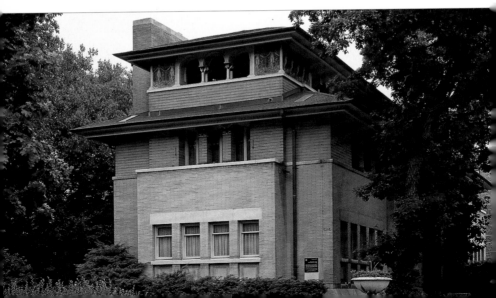

FREDERICK C ROBIE HOUSE
5757 South Woodlawn Avenue
Chicago 60637
1909 0908

GPS: N 41 47.399
         W 87 35.795

Directions: Exit Lake Shore Drive at 55th Street and turn past and around the Museum of Science and Industry to 60th Street. Turn west down the Midway Plaisance 0.6 miles to Woodlawn and turn north. The house is two blocks north on Woodlawn Avenue at the northeast corner with 58th Street.

Accessibility: The house can be seen from the street. The Robie House is under a new restoration and tour program through the Frank LLoyd Wright Home and Studio Foundation. It is expected that the 'tours at noon' will continue and perhaps be expanded.

■ An engineering graduate of Purdue University, Robie was an automobile, bicycle and motorcycle manufacturer. Born in 1879, he met his future wife, Laura, at a dance at the University of Chicago. He continued to court her after she returned to Springfield, Illinois, where they were married in 1902. He worked for his father's Excelsior Supply Company and took it over upon his father's death in 1910. In 1912, the company made large losses and was bought out by Schwinn. After the company failed, his marriage broke down and he moved out of this house after only two years. It was the love of automobiles that linked

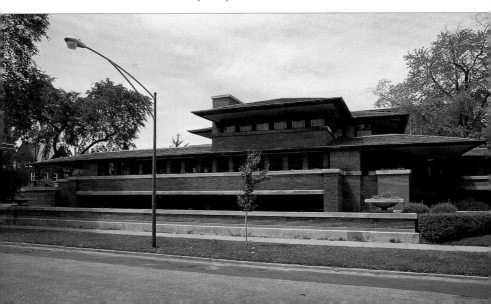

Robie and Wright. Robie contacted Wright at Christmas time in 1906 concerning the commission after showing some of his sketches for a house to several contractors and being told that what he wanted was, 'one of those damned Wright houses.'

The Robie House is on a lot 60 x 180 feet facing south. The entry is not easy to locate as it is on the house's north side. The land cost $13,500, the building $35,000 and the furnishings $10,000, totaling $58,500 in all. This compares to the $4,700 Wright paid for his own house twenty years earlier and the $20,000 that the Winslow and the Willits Houses each cost.

Now the furniture and carpets have been substituted with near copies. Some of the original furniture is in the University of Chicago's Smart Museum to the northwest of the Robie House and the cantilever couch is in the Metropolitan Museum, New York. c76

(On the southwest corner of Cottage Grove Avenue and 60th Street is the site of Midway Gardens, Opus #1401. Built in 1914 this open-air beer garden was demolished in 1929, after the onset of Prohibition that caused its business to evaporate. The story goes, after several demolition contractors went broke tearing down such a well-built structure, the rubble, along with most of the Ianelli-designed sprites, were used as landfill in nearby Lake Michigan. The Wallers, see p49, owned Midway Gardens along with partner John Vogelsang, who also commissioned another garden setting for dining and entertainment, Opus# 1407, the same year.

Along the Midway and east at Jackson Park is the site of the 1893 World's Fair, which contained Sullivan's Transportation Building, the Japanese Pavilion and the Turkish Pavilion. The Japanese Pavilion gave many Chicago architects their first opportunity to see Japanese architecture. The design of the Turkish Pavilion was very similar to that of the Winslow House, p52.)

WILLIAM ADAMS HOUSE
9326 South Pleasant Avenue
Chicago 60620
1900 0001

GPS: N 41 43.483
       W 87 40.183

Directions: Exit Interstate 94 at 95th Street, US Route 12/20, and drive west 2.4 miles to Damen. Drive north to 93rd Street then east two blocks to Pleasant Avenue which is one-way southbound. Turn north two blocks to the house on the west side of the street.

Accessibility: The house can be seen from the street.

■ Adams was the contractor for the Husser and Heller Houses (pp114 and 124). No one has located Adams's descendants but it is vital that his papers for these three houses that he built are found. The house has double-hung windows, which is most likely a client request. This is a simple house in the manner of the Emmond and Goan Houses (pp104 and 105). c95

RAYMOND W EVANS HOUSE
9914 South Longwood Drive
Chicago 60643
1908 0805

GPS: N 41 42.791
       W 87 40.170

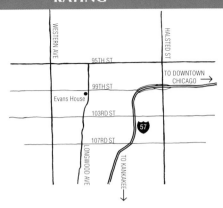

Directions: Exit Interstate 57 at Halsted Street and drive west for a mile to Longwood Drive. Turn south and the house is on the west side of the street, second from the corner.

Accessibility: The house can be seen from the street, though there is no parking at that point.

■ The synthetic stone facing is not original to the construction. The central, two-story pavilion of the house is a near duplicate of the Hunt House (p106) with the living room taking up half the area of the first floor. There was a full set of furniture built for the house. Most of it has been located and is now in museums across the United States.   c96

BURHANS-ELLINWOOD & CO MODEL HOUSE
(American Systems House)
10410 South Hoyne Avenue
Chicago 60643
1917 1506

GPS: N 41 42.281
W 87 40.444

Directions: Continue south on Longwood Drive to 103rd Street and turn west. Drive 1.2 miles to Hoyne Avenue and turn south to the house on the west side of the street.

Accessibility: The house can be seen from the street.

■ American Systems (see also p79, UGL) employed novelist Sherwood Anderson as their copywriter when he worked for Taylor, Crithfield, Clague Company, a Chicago advertising firm. This house, with offices in the neighborhood for Burhans, Ellinwood & Company (the agent for Richards Company in Milwaukee, who produced the houses), was used in a full-page advertisement in the *Chicago Tribune* to promote these designs by the contractor PD Diamond & Co. The building permit was taken out on 17 July 1917 and construction was completed in December. It was originally built as a model for the proposed development and sold to, the first owner, Mr Smith in 1920.   c95

H HOWARD HYDE HOUSE
(American Systems House)
10541 South Hoyne Avenue
Chicago 60643
1917 1506

GPS: N 41 42.137
W 87 40.424

Directions: Continue south on Longwood Drive to 103rd Street and turn west. Drive 1.2 miles and turn south to the house on the east side of the street.

Accessibility: The house can be seen from the street.

■ This is a virtual duplicate of a house that has been found recently in Iowa (see West volume). The idea was that all the lumber would be precut, labeled and shipped to the site. The building plans would indicate where each board would be placed. Hyde was a cashier for the International Harvester Company, owned by the McCormick family. The building permit was taken out by the contractor PD Diamond on 16 May 1917.

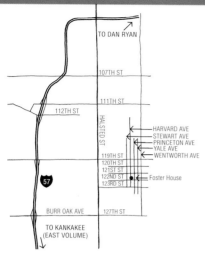

STEPHEN A FOSTER HOUSE
12147 South Harvard Avenue
Chicago 60628
1900 0003

GPS: N 41 40.352
       W 87 37.847

Directions: Exit Interstate 57 at 119th Street and drive east one mile to Halsted (800 west) and turn south for three blocks to 122nd Street and follow it to the house. The house is on the corner of 122nd Street and Harvard. Harvard is not a continuous street.

Accessibility: The house can be seen from the street.

■ This is a rare Japanese-inspired house for attorney, later Judge, Foster. He lived in the house less than twenty years. It recently became a Chicago Landmark. The house is certainly one of the most unique of Wright's career. The garage is also Wright's design and was featured in an elaborate drawing of the house.

JAMES CHARNLEY HOUSE
by Adler & Sullivan
1365 Astor Street
Chicago 60610
1891 9001

GPS: N 41 54.802
     W 87 37.671

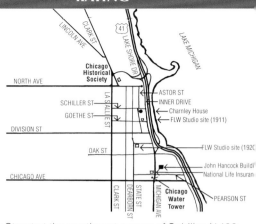

Directions: The house is east of State Street at the southeast corner of Schiller (1400 north) and Astor, one block west of inner Lake Shore Drive.

Accessibility: The house can be seen from the street. If one calls ahead, a tour can be arranged with the Society of Architectural Historians, the building's occupants. Phone 312-573-1365.

■ Charnley owned a lumber company. He also had land in Mississippi along the Gulf Coast and commissioned Louis Sullivan to design a winter house there. Charnley sold a part of this property to Sullivan for his winter vacation house. The story is that Wright was given the job to design this residence as the firm was concentrating on commercial commissions. In the 1990s, Seymour Persky provided funding for the Society of Architectural Historians to acquire the house and use it as their national headquarters.

NEAR NORTH SITES
See maps on pp132 and 136.

FRANK LLOYD WRIGHT STUDIO SITE, Goethe Street
1911 1113

■ After his return from Europe in 1911, Wright understood that he would need a city site for some of his business activities and designed this townhouse with a small architectural office. Its exact address is still unknown and the property records are unclear as to Wright's ownership. The plan is reminiscent of the Italian buildings Wright visited while abroad.

FLW APARTMENT AND PROPOSED STUDIO, Cedar Street
1920s

■ Wright maintained an apartment at 19 East Cedar after building Taliesin and resided here while he became involved with Miriam Noel. He announced his intention to open a Chicago studio next door at 25 East Cedar from January 1925, but the move never took place. It was probably because the National Life Insurance Building failed to materialize.

NATIONAL LIFE INSURANCE BUILDING, Water Tower Square
1924 2404

■ Albert Mussey Johnson was born in Oberlin, Ohio, on 31 May 1872. He worked for Arkansas Midland Railroad and the family business Mussey Stone Co in Elyria, Ohio, as well as for the Missouri lead and zinc mines before coming to Chicago in 1902. In 1929, he became Chairman of the Board of National Life Insurance Co. Johnson lived in a lakefront, Prairie-style house at Devon Avenue on 6353 Sheridan Road. Alfred MacArthur (1885-1967) of Oak Park, who had been the publisher of the Oak Park *Oak Leaves* with his brother Telefer, joined the insurance company in 1907. Alfred brought his brother John D into the company where he prospered, leaving his money to the MacArthur Foundation. In 1915 Alfred purchased Wright's Forest Avenue home and rented it to another brother, Charles, a playwright and co-writer of *The Front Page* with Ben Hecht.

In about 1921, Albert Johnson hired Wright to carry out some design work for Death Valley, California. It went largely unbuilt.

Wright's design for the this building was copper and glass, and twenty-four stories high. An earlier scheme, dated 1921 to 1923, was produced by Graham Anderson Probst & White of Chicago. The drawings are at the Burnham Library, Art Institute of Chicago.

MILE HIGH ILLINOIS, Lincoln Park
1956 5617

■ This was Wright's proposal for a multi-use building situated near the south border of Lincoln Park at North Avenue. It was to have 528 floors, house 130,000 people, 15,000 cars and 150 helicopters. In recent years the Otis Elevator Co announced that it had a design which could make this building feasible. The Mile High would have been four times taller than the Sears Tower.

FINE ARTS BUILDING SITES, 410 South Michigan Avenue
BROWNES BOOKSTORE SITE, Suite 706
1907 0802

■ The opening of the bookstore was announced on 16 November 1907 in *The Dial*, the literary journal owned by the Brownes. Five years earlier, in 1902, Wright had designed some offices for magazine (Opus #0218), but these had remained unrealized. The bookstore had a short life. It was demolished in April 1912. Many accessory pieces were included in this interior, which are now found elsewhere. They include the copper weed holders and urn, art-glass chandeliers and a full compliment of custom furniture. A few pieces of furniture, such as the tall back chairs, emerged in Unity Temple.

The Caxton Club had offices and meeting rooms on the tenth floor. In 1895, it was organized by Chauncey Williams and George Millard among others. Members included Wright (1907-10), Martin Ryerson, George Armour, Daniel Burnham, Joseph Lyman Silsbee and Ralph Fletcher Seymour. In 1908 and 1910, after his return from Europe, Wright had his offices here in suite 1020.

THURBER ART GALLERY SITE, 5th Floor
1909 0911

■ This was a scheme similar in many ways to the Brownes Bookstore with alcoves and custom furniture although it was much larger. It was the first to have a backless chair similar to the Coonley House end table that was lower and cushioned. The ceiling art glass was quite like that in the gallery of the Barnsdall House, a type of ladder arrangement. It was demolished in 1917.

MORI ART SHOP SITE, Suite 801
1914 1402

■ The fourth and last of the interiors for the Fine Arts Building was on the eighth floor. The art shop remained in business until its last owner, Mary Diamond, closed it in the early 1960s. In the 1970s, some of the small end tables and display cases were presented to the University of Illinois at Chicago and then given to the Frank Lloyd Wright Home and Studio Foundation.

FRANK LLOYD WRIGHT OFFICES, STEINWAY HALL SITE,
64 East ven Buren Street

■ Steinway Hall was built in 1896 and was designed by Dwight H Perkins with Professor Lewis J Johnson as the engineer. It was eleven stories and 158 feet tall. Perkins rented the loft and part of the top floor. He shared these offices with Wright, Robert C Spencer, Cecil Corwin, Myron Hunt, Webster Tomlinson and Walter Burley Griffin. Wright had his office here in 1897 and again between 1901 and 1907.

(From 1893 until 1896, after leaving Adler & Sullivan, Wright shared an office in the Garrick Theater, also known as the Schiller Building, with Cecil Corwin. The building was designed by his previous employer as was the Borden Block east of it. In 1915, Wright had offices in Orchestra Hall. The tenth floor of the building was the home the Cliff Dwellers' Club and Sullivan in his last few years.)

ROOKERY BUILDING LOBBY
209 South La Salle Street
Chicago 60604
1905 0511

GPS: N 87 37.918
       W 41 52.752

Directions: The Rookery is located at the southeast corner of Adams and La Salle Street.

Accessibility: The building is open during regular business hours. The Chicago Architecture Foundation gives a Loop tour that includes the Rookery Building. The lobby is generally open between 8.00am and 6.00pm.

■ Wright's work here appears to date from much earlier than 1905. Perhaps the design was executed just after 1897 when Wright had his offices here and he and Edward Waller (see p49), the building's manager, were involved with the Luxfer Prism Company. The building was designed in 1886 by Waller's friend Daniel Burnham of Burnham & Root, who had built his own house for him (p49).

In 1898-99, Wright's office was located here on the eleventh floor. It was next door to the offices for the Luxfer Prism Company, where Waller was an officer.

The building and the lobby were recently restored by McClier Co.   c96

THE AUDITORIUM
by Adler & Sullivan
430 South Michigan Avenue
Chicago 60605

GPS: N 41 52.518
　　　 W 87 37.538
UTM: 16 T 044 8126
　　　 463 6120

Directions: The Auditorium is at the northwest corner of Congress and Michigan.

Accessibility: The building is open regularly.

■ The Auditorium Building (in the center of the photograph with the Fine Arts Building on the right) was already on the firm's drawing boards when Wright joined Adler & Sullivan in about 1887. After the completion of this first multi-function building, which included an office building, luxury hotel and acoustically perfect auditorium, the Adler & Sullivan offices were relocated from their earlier Borden Block to the sixteenth-floor tower. Sullivan had the southeast corner and Wright shared an office with George Grant Elmslie in the northeast corner.

The performance auditorium is now operated by a separate company from that of the rest of the building, which is part of Roosevelt University. The Banquet Hall is a library and the bar has been demolished.

Belvidere

Pettit Chapel, open everyday that the cemetery is open.

Chicago

Auditorium Building, stage shows and other entertainment are available at the Auditorium Theater. Roosevelt University operates the other parts of the building as a school. Much of it is open to the public. There are tours of it from time to time.

Charnley House, tours arranged by the Society of Architectural Historians (SAH). Call 312/915-0105.

Graceland Cemetery, Sullivan Grave, open everyday from 8.30am to 4.00pm.

Robie House, contact the Frank Lloyd Wright Home and Studio Foundation for information. Call 708/848-1976.

Rookery Building, is open every working day. Tours are conducted here by the Chicago Architecture Foundation.

Rosehill Cemetery, Catherine Lloyd Wright Grave, is open everyday from 8.30am to 4.00pm.

Geneva

Fabyan House, owned by the Kane County Forest Preserve District and administered by the Friends of Fabyan. Access to the site is open everyday. Tours of the interiors are available. Call 630/232-4811.

Oak Park

Cheney House, now open as a Bed & Breakfast establishment. Bookings only taken by reservation in advance. Call Dale Smirl 708/524-2067.

Horse Show Association Foundation is in a public park and is accessible at all times.

Nathan Moore House, tours are administered by the Oak Park Tour Center located on Forest Avenue near Lake Street.

Frank Lloyd Wright Home and Studio, tours everyday with the annual Wright Plus Tour on the third Saturday in every May. Call 708/843-1976.

Unity Temple, regular tours are available. Call 708/383-8873.

■ Tour information can be obtained through the Chicago Architecture Foundation (phone 312/922-8687). They give over fifty tours in and around Chicago. The Oak Park Visitors' Center is another good source of information (708/848-1500), as is the Frank Lloyd Wright Home and Studio Foundation (708/848-1976). Some of these organizations also have web sites on the Internet, which supply further information on Frank Lloyd Wright and his buildings.

■ The first buildings of architectural interest that I ever saw were three designed by Walter Burley Griffin. They are the two Comstock Houses and the Bovee House in Evanston. I passed them frequently by car while I was in high school. I drove around most of the North Shore looking at buildings (though I missed several Wright designs by a block or two and did not locate them until Al Drap gave me the addresses).

In 1971 Al Drap (an architect from Fort Smith, Arkansas), Steve Barnes and another undergraduate from the University of Illinois, Urbana, and I took our first trip to Chicago to visit Frank Lloyd Wright buildings. We visited the Robie House on Chicago's south side. The excitement built as we turned off the Midway onto Woodlawn. All of us were surprised by the house after seeing it in countless photographs. Looking back, they were the same two black and white photographs seen countless times. The context of the house in the neighborhood is what surprised me. I had always thought of it as being on a very wide lot, perhaps even taking up the entire block. When I saw the house up against the sidewalk on a very tight corner it seemed like it was in the wrong place. Looking at it, the house seemed much smaller that I had imagined, but walking up to the front wall and seeing that the flower urns were nearly six feet wide gave me a very different perspective. Was it small with large pieces?

All of us were students of Walter Creese, Professor of Architectural History at the University of Illinois and one of the founders of the Society of Architectural Historians. He gave us insights into Wright's work in the classes he taught. Many other professors had comments to make about Wright and his work but none encouraged us to visit these treasures, and there were no field trips arranged by the school to visit the buildings we had seen and studied in class. Al and I started our own program of annual fall and spring trips. We always did research about the areas that we were visiting and took a small library with us. This is the best way to understand buildings.

Paul Sprague's office in Glessner House was a place that was always filled with the excitement of exploration. At that time he was heading the Illinois Historic Structures Survey. Every town in Illinois was visited by his field personnel and every building of interest was photographed and noted. The photos were then mounted on note cards and analyzed. Guesses were made as to the architect, date and other information. This was architectural history in action. It was exciting to discover an unknown work by Walter Burley Griffin or see a great Joseph Lyman Silsbee house. Sprague was teaching at the University of Chicago and was President of the Chicago Chapter of the Society of Architectural Historians. The SAH took frequent trips around the Midwest to see buildings, such as one to Quincy where we saw two Silsbee houses and others in the Prairie style done by another local architect, as well as some HH Richardson-style commercial buildings and a large house by Spencer & Powers with a mantle by Orlando Giannini. I met scores of other architectural enthusiasts who also enjoyed visiting these fascinating but little-known architectural treasures.

On one of these trips I was lucky enough to meet the Chicago expert on Wright at that time, Don Kalec. We spent hundreds of hours together, talking about Wright's work and visiting his houses. Don's insights and vast understanding of the buildings spurred me on to learn more.

Alice Sinkevitch, who became the Director of the ArchiCenter for the Chicago Architecture Foundation and is now the Executive Director of the AIA Chicago, showed me a great deal about writing and researching during the short time that we worked together on a small publication. Her writing is so good, it is a shame that she does not do it full time. She is also an expert on the architecture of Oak Park and Chicago having edited the *AIA Guide to Chicago*.

While involved with Frank Lloyd Wright's Home and Studio, I became acquainted with several other outstanding people, including Gay Pearson Anderson, Carla Lind, John Thorpe and Bob Bell. They have all been very helpful in revealing many things about Wright and his work.

I became acquainted with the late Lloyd Wright and his son, Eric, during my many trips to Los Angeles and their trips to Oak Park to consult on the Studio. Both of them have been most kind and patient in answering my many mundane questions.

I met Narcisco Menocal while he was a graduate student at the University of Illinois preparing his PhD on Louis Sullivan. We toured Chicago together looking at Sullivan buildings. Through the years he and I have had many interesting discussions on a wide range of subjects. He and his family were gracious hosts when I took the four-day architectural exam in Wisconsin.

Walter L Creese in many ways is my mentor. He helped get me through his architectural history courses at Illinois. I don't think I got more than a B in any one of them. With his lists, I went and saw the buildings first hand. This was inspirational. The slides identified the structure, but with my notes and my immediate experience of the buildings, I understood the significance of his statements. I worked with him on his book, *The Eight Great Spaces of America*. I learned another way to see and think about the coming together of man and nature. He always imparts a highly perceptive view of architecture and particular historical situations. I thank him for that.

Bruce Goff was a great friend. He would talk for many hours on the phone and in person about the buildings he had seen and built. I miss him. Allan Brooks and Norris Kelly Smith both came to Chicago for the SAH and as guests of the Frank Lloyd Wright Studio. I was able to pick them up at the airport and take them around Chicago and Oak Park. Both were great teachers in this way.

Jack Prost allowed me to live in the lower story of the Heurtley House for a couple of years. Bill and Jackie Dugal have located a tremendous amount of information about Moore and his family and are making it available while giving tours of their wonderful house. Bill and Janet Dring allowed me to spend many hours in their home studying and photographing. Bob Coleman of the Thomas House kept me up to date as he was restoring it. Mr and Mrs Bloch of the Booth House were very helpful and gracious with their time. The Willits House owner, Sakip Altay, allowed me to take X-rays of important structural components and to study the mechanical systems that were once used. The

Finebergs of the Glassner House were always eager to share their home. Claire and Juan Montenegro have been very enthusiastic and kind in allowing me to learn more about the Millard House. The Bartons were always available, even on short notice to open the WE Martin House when I called. Dale Smirl of the Cheney House has amassed the largest collection of Heritage-Henredon Wright-designed furniture and displays it in the Cheney House Bed and Breakfast to lucky visitors that can get a reservation. The Walkers, who treasure the Winslow House, keep it in pristine condition. Ellis and Jeanette Fields have always encouraged scholarship in every way and are some of the most conscientious owners. Maya Moran has finally published her life story as told through her experiences with the Tomek House. Nick and the late Mary Sahlas of the Coonley House went through great pains in rebuilding the house after the terrible fire that struck it. Ann and Ed Marcisz of the Hunt House were always excited to show me what they had discovered. It was a pleasure to visit them. I am grateful to Alice Shaddle for allowing me to live in the Blossom House garage for several months. Many thanks to all the owners who really made this and the other books possible.

Jack Howe and I toured around Evanston, his boyhood home. He explained in detail the buildings that his Uncle Hebert, Wright's dentist, owned, and identified the work that was done to them.

Sandra L Williams of the Hinsdale Historical Society and Kelley Gibson who lives in a beautiful Arts and Crafts/Prairie house in Hinsdale helped in the research of the W Freeman House. Tom Rickard of Tacoma, Washington, is a gifted researcher and finder of facts. He has helped to discover many important facts about Wright buildings. John Eifler assisted with information concerning the Waller Apartments and the Brown House. Tim Samuelson is a walking encyclopedia of architectural history. His information always solves the mystery. Susan Benjamin and Susan Sollway showed me their research on many of the Glencoe buildings. They discovered the lost train station that Sherman Booth built. It is hoped that they will publish their work in book form soon. Tina Wayne, the assistant to the Village Manager of Glencoe, brought out all of the building permits and water bills for me to examine besides answering my many questions by phone. Jack Randall was of considerable help with many of the Glencoe properties. Chris Meyers located the two Wright designs in Gary, and I connected him with Seymour Persky who owns the Mahoney rendering of the Moe house for confirmation of the design. Bruce and Yoshiko Smith, publishers of *The Tabby*, have been important in helping to get this publication in this form. David De Long was of assistance in giving proper names to the Booth and American Systems buildings. Jonathan Lipman, Sara-Ann Briggs and Tammy Way of the Frank Lloyd Wright Building Conservancy were helpful in information and the naming process.

Mrs Wright, Bruce Brooks Pfeiffer, the late Wes Peters, Oscar Munoz, Margo Stipe and many others at The Frank Lloyd Wright Foundation have been helpful recently and over the past twenty years in assisting me with the research for this and other books.

At the Ricker Library, Al and I nearly wore out a copy of Hitchcock's book and nearly the patience of the librarians with our constant inquiries. At the Burnham Library, Annette Fern and Mary Woolever have gone out of their way to explore my many requests, as has Barbara Ballenger, the Head Librarian of Oak Park Public Library for many years. Thank you for your help. Mariam Touba, Reference Librarian at The New-York Historical Society, has helped with some background information about Cecil Corwin.

At Academy Editions, John Stoddart, Maggie Toy, Andrea Bettella and Mira Joka have had the vision to see that everything can be improved upon. Thanks also to Helen Castle for her editorial assistance. Marianne Bohr is, as always, eager and supportive with her comments and suggestions. Her work has helped to shape these volumes.

Jack Hedrich of Hedrich-Blessing and Balthazar Korab have been very encouraging with their knowledge and assistance in the world of photography.

Northwestern University Map Library assisted with their full set of Geological Survey maps. Discussions with Jerry Jones formerly of Rand McNally were always informative.

My family is a constant source of inspiration. After every trip, they would always put up with my little slide shows shown on the dining-room wall. Only my youngest brother, John, actually watched with any interest. Ann Terando has been helpful in many ways. Thank you to all.

Sprites from the now demolished Midway Gardens, Chicago, Ill, c 1914

BOOKS

■ *The Book of Chicagoans*, AN Marquis (Chicago).
The predecessors of the Who's Who series by the same publisher. Like the later series, they contain short biographical entries on significant people. Many of Wright's clients and friends are listed. First issued in 1905, with volumes following in 1911, 1917, etc.

■ Arthur Drexler, *The Drawings of Frank Lloyd Wright*, Horizon Press (New York).

■ John Drury, *Old Chicago Houses*, University of Chicago Press (Chicago), 1941.
This is a compilation of vignettes on historic houses.

■ Henry-Russell Hitchcock, *In the Nature of Materials*, Duell, Sloan & Pearce (New York), 1942.
With the last twenty years of work missing, it is still the best single volume on Wright. The list of buildings is consistently the most accurate. It remains a most valuable resource.

■ Sidney Kramer, *A History of Stone & Kimball and Herbert S. Stone & Co. 1893-1905*, The University of Chicago Press (Chicago), 1944.
This book not only covers Stone and his family – a sister, Elizabeth, was another possible Wright client from Glencoe – but also other clients of Wright.

■ John Replinger and Allan Frumkin, *Buildings by Frank Lloyd Wright in Six Middle Western States: Illinois, Indiana, Iowa, Michigan, Minnesota, Wisconsin*, The Art Institute of Chicago (Chicago), 1949.
Based upon Hitchcock's 1942 list, it has valuable and updated information, but also misses the last ten years of Wright's output. A small publication, not in general circulation.

■ Frank A Randall, *History of Chicago Buildings*, University of Illinois Press (Urbana, Illinois), 1949.
One of the most remarkable reference books on Chicago's commercial buildings. It includes an amazing amount of data and locations for both the famous and the lesser buildings.
It may appear in an updated version in the next few years.

■ Edgar Kaufmann (ed), *Taliesin Drawings*, Wittenborn Schultz Inc (New York), 1952.

■ Grant Carpenter Manson, *Frank Lloyd Wright to 1910*, Reinhold Publishing (New York), 1957.
One of the seminal works on Wright's early buildings, most of which were built in the MetroChicago area. It still yields important information expecially in the appendices.

■ Edgar Kaufmann and Ben Raeburn (eds), *Frank Lloyd Wright: Writings and Buildings*, Meridian Books, New York, 1960.
Besides essential material on the published writings, it has the earliest list of works.

■ Leonard K Eaton, *Two Chicago Architects and their Clients*, MIT Press (Cambridge, Mass), 1969.
Short biographies of several of Wright's clients are presented.

■ Wayne Andrews, *Architecture in Chicago and Midwest*, Athenaeum (New York), 1970.
A chapter is devoted to Wright and a few others associated with the Prairie School. The views are more casual and give information usually not found in other publications.

■ H Allen Brooks, *The Prairie School: Frank Lloyd Wright and his Midwest Contemporaries*, University of Toronto Press (Toronto), 1972.
Allen Brooks presents the finest work on the buildings of Wright and others associated with him. A good account of how the new American architecture grew and died.

■ Paul E Sprague, *Guide to Frank Lloyd Wright and Prairie School Architecture in Oak Park,* Oak Park Bicentennial and Landmarks Commissions (Chicago), 1976.
This small book contains maps and discussions of important landmarks in Oak Park.

■ Julia M Ehresmann (ed), *Geneva, Illinois: A History of Its Times and Places*, Geneva Public Library District (Chicago), 1977.
A very good book that includes information on the Hoyt House; Ralph Fletcher Seymour, the publisher; and a full chapter on Colonel Fabyan and the work at his estate.

■ Robert L Sweeney, *Frank Lloyd Wright: An Annotated Bibliography*, Hennessey & Ingalls (Los Angeles), 1978.
Virtually every publication on Wright and his buildings is noted in this excellent work. There is an index by building name for those interested in more historical background. One wishes that an updated volume might be forthcoming.

■ Brian A Spencer (ed), *The Prairie School Tradition*, AIA, Whitney Library of Design, Watson-Guptil Publications (New York), 1979.

■ Robert C Twombly, *Frank Lloyd Wright, his Life and his Architecture*, John Wiley & Sons (New York), 1979.
A second edition of the interpretive biography that blazed new trails in discovering the reality of Wright's life and work.

■ Jeanette Fields (ed), *A Guidebook to the Architecture of River Forest*, River Forest Community Center (Chicago), 1981.

■ Anthony Alofsin (ed), *Frank Lloyd Wright: An Index to the Taliesin Correspondence*, Garland Press (New York), 1983.
The microfilmed letters to and from Frank Lloyd Wright are indexed and cross-referenced within these five volumes. Bruce Brooks Pfeiffer, the Taliesin Archivist has compiled the definitive list of all of the work of Frank Lloyd Wright.

■ Patrick J Meehan, *Frank Lloyd Wright: A Guide to Archival Sources*, Garland (New York), 1983.
Listing not only the locations of the archival sources but also fine summaries of the contents of each, this book is not widely known.

■ Donald Hoffmann, *Frank Lloyd Wright's Robie House*, Dover Publications (New York), 1984.
A great publication that goes into enormous detail about Robie, the construction of the house, and the subsequent owners.

■ Joseph Connors, *The Robie House of Frank Lloyd Wright*, University of Chicago Press (Chicago), 1984.
A good casual discussion of thes Robie House in a wider context.

■ Walter L Creese, *The Crowning of the American Landscape: Eight Great Spaces and their Buildings,* Princeton University Press (Princeton, New Jersey), 1985.
This provides new information about the history of Riverside and Graceland Cemetery.

■ Scott Elliott, *Frank Lloyd Wright and Viollet-le-Duc*, Kelmscott Gallery (Chicago), 1986.
An exhibition catalogue of the work of the two designers with many previously unpublished photographs. A chapter gives short biographies of many of the participants in the movement, including Marion Mahoney, Alfonso Ianelli and Emile Gallé.

■ Robert Twombly, *Louis Sullivan, his Life and Work*, Viking Penguin (New York), 1986.
This book uncovers much new material, which explains many mysteries in Sullivan's life and the details of his last years, as well as his relationship with Wright.

■ Henry Regnery, *The Cliff Dwellers*, Chicago Historical Bookworks (Evanston, Illinois), 1990.
The Cliff Dewllers' Club is best known for harboring Louis Sullivan in his last years. It was and is still instrumental in fostering the interchange between artists and patrons.

■ Miles L Berger, *They Built Chicago*, Bonus Books (Chicago), 1992.
This book focuses on the clients of the important buildings and projects in Chicago, such as Edward C Waller, Ferdinand Peck, J Lewis Cochran and Robert A Waller.

■ Alice Sinkevitch (ed), *AIA Guide to Chicago*, Harcourt, Brace & Co (San Diego, New York, London), 1993
A great book for learning more about the locations of the great buildings of Chicago. One wishes that it covered more of the suburban communities – possibly in the second edition.

■ Henry Regnery, *Creative Chicago*, Chicago Historical Bookworks (Evanston, Illinois), 1993.
The creators of Chicago are examined from a literary standpoint along with the authors and publishers of books and periodicals like *The Chap Book* and *The Dial*. Clients of Wright are prominent figures in these ventures.

■ Mary Jane Hamilton, *Frank Lloyd Wright and the Book Arts*, Friends of the University of Wisconsin-Madison Libraries (Madison, Wisconsin), 1993.
A great book that links many of the clients and other personalities with whom Wright surrounded himself by focusing on their literary connections.

■ William Allin Storrer, *The Frank Lloyd Wright Companion*, University of Chicago Press (Chicago and London), 1993.
A considerable amount of work went into the assembly of this book. It tries to show plans for every Wright building ever built. Mr Storrer has included a lot of information on many little-known clients as well as architectural commentary.

■ Timothy Samuelson, *American System-Built Houses; Staff Summary of Information*, Commission on Chicago Landmarks, 1 December 1993.
This is a very well-written and researched document concerning the Burhans & Ellinwod & Co Model House and the H Howard Hyde House in Chicago.

■ Neil Levine, *The Architecture of Frank Lloyd Wright*, Princeton University Press (Princeton, New Jersey), 1996.
A few major works are highlighted and discussed in great detail. Mr Levine's discussions bring into the analysis many lesser designs.

■ Susan Solway and Susan Benjamin, *Ravine Bluffs Bridge*, United States Department of the Interior, Historic American Engineering Record (HAER), Prints and Photographs Division, (Library of Congress, Washington, DC), no IL-14, 1996.
This publication includes nearly all of Wright's Glencoe designs, as well as the bridge.

■ William C Gannett, *The House Beautiful*, John Arthur Edition, 1996.
This was printed and bound originally by William H Winslow and Frank Lloyd Wright in 1896. A beautiful reprint of this rare original. It also includes an important text by Gannett.

■ Carla Lind, *Lost Wright*, Simon & Schuster (New York), 1996.
This covers many of Wright's buildings that have been destroyed by neglect or fire.

■ Joseph M Siry, *Unity Temple*, Cambridge University Press (Cambridge, New York & Melbourne), 1996.
Nearly everything that one would want to know about this masterpiece is contained in this work. Construction and engineering techniques are discussed at length. There should be more books like this one.

PERIODICALS

■ Leonard K Eaton, 'W. H. Winslow and the Winslow House,' *The Prairie School Review*, vol 1, no 3, Third Quarter, 1964, pp12-14.
This short article by Hasbrouck, and another unsigned, discusses the Winslow House. There are some good early photographs.

■ Griggs, Joseph, 'Alfonso Ianelli, The Prairie Spirit in Sculpture,' *The Priarie School Review*, vol 2, no 4, Fourth Quarter, 1965, pp5-23.
The collaboration between Wright and Ianelli on Midway Gardens is discussed.

■ Wilbert R Hasbrouck, 'Frederick C. Robie House, Frank Lloyd Wright, Architect,' *The Prairie School Review*, vol 4, no 4, Fourth Quarter, 1967, pp 10-19.
The recent restoration by SOM and some of the history of the house is featured.

■ Susan Karr Sorell, 'Silsbee: The Evolution of a Personal Architectural Style,' and Wilber R Hasbrouck, 'The earliest Work of Frank Lloyd Wright', *The Prairie School Review*, vol 7, no 4, Fourth Quarter, 1970, pp5-13 and 17-21 for Silsbee, and pp14-16 for Wright.
Two very short articles provide good research about both subjects with some illustrations.

■ Donald P Hallmark, 'Richard W. Bock, Sculptor Part II: The Mature Collaborations,' *The Prairie School Review*, vol 8, no 2, Second Quarter, 1971, pp5-29.

■ *Frank Lloyd Wright Newsletter*, vol 1, no 3, May 1978.
An article on the discovery of several unknown Wright buildings.

■ Charney, Wayne Michael, 'The W. I. Clark House, La Grange Illinois,' *Frank Lloyd Wright Newsletter*, vol 1, no 3, May 1978, pp4-8.
A detailed discussion of the long-misattributed house.

■ Robert L Sweeney, 'The Coonley Playhouse, Riverside, Illinois,' *Frank Lloyd Wright Newsletter*, vol 1, no 6, November 1978, pp2-4.
Information gathered, in part, from an interview with Coonley's daughter.

■ Mark David Linch, 'Ward Winfield Willits, A Client of Frank LLoyd Wright,' *Frank Lloyd Wright Newsletter*, Part I, vol 2, no 2, First Quarter, 1979, pp12-17; Part II, vol 2, no 3, Second Quarter, 1979, pp1-5; Part III, vol 3, no 1, First Quarter, 1980, pp7-11.
This three-part article discusses Willits and the design and construction of the masterpiece.

■ Strauss, Irma, 'An Interview with Lorraine Robie O'Connor,' *Frank Lloyd Wright Newsletter*, vol 3, no 4, Fourth Quarter, 1980, pp1-3.
A revealing interview between the late Irma Strauss and Robie's daughter.

■ Gay L Pearson, ' The Muirhead House: An Interview with Robert and Betty Muirhead,' *Frank Lloyd Wright Newsletter*, vol 4, no 1, First Quarter, 1981, pp1-4.
A well-written, insightful interview with original clients.

■ Susan Solway, 'Frank Lloyd Wright and Glencoe,' *Wright Angles: The Newsletter of the Frank Lloyd Wright Home and Studio Foundation*, vol 19, no 3, 1993, pp3-6.
This is the first time the Booth Train Station was published.

E Arthur Davenport House with its original porch, River Forest, Ill, c 1901

This is a full list of the proposed, existing and demolished buildings that appear in the Frank Lloyd Wright Guides.

Key	Volume Name
UGL	Upper Great Lakes
W	West
E	East
MC	MetroChicago

Wynant, Wilber, Gary, Ind.	MC	1916	1506	109
Anderton Court, Los Angeles, Beverly Hills, Calif.	W	1952	5032	
Angster, Herbert, Lake Bluff, Ill, site.	MC	1911	1101	18
Annunciation Greek Orthodox Church, Wauwatosa, Wisc.	UGL	1956	5611	83
Anthony, Howard E, Benton Harbor, Mich.	UGL	1949	4901	131
Arizona Biltmore Hotel, Phoenix, Ariz.	W	1927	2710	
Armstrong, Andrew F, Ogden Dunes, Ind.	MC	1939	3901	111
Arnold, E Clarke, Columbus, Wisc.	UGL	1954	5401	66
Auldbrass, Stevens Plantation, Yemassee, SC.	E	1940	4015	
Austin, Charlcey, Greenville, SC.	E	1951	5102	
Bach, Emil, Chicago, Ill.	MC	1915	1501	115
Baghdad Projects, Iraq. site	W	1957	5748	
Bagley, Frederick, Hinsdale, Ill.	MC	1894	9401	101
Bagley, Joseph J, Grand Beach, Mich.	UGL	1916	1601	134
Baird, Theodore, Amherst, Mass.	E	1940	4001	
Baker, Frank J, Wilmette, Ill.	MC	1909	0901	36
Balch, Oscar B, Oak Park, Ill.	MC	1911	1102	80
Baldwin, Hiram, Kenilworth, Ill.	MC	1905	0502	35
Banff National Park Pavilion, Canada, site	W	1911	1302	
Bannerstone House – see Dana, Susan Lawrence.	E	1904	9905	
Barnsdall, Aline, Hollyhock House, Los Angeles, Calif.	W	1920	1705	
Kindergarten, Little Dipper.	W	1921	2301	
Studio Residence A.	W	1920	2002	
Studio Residence B, site.	W	1920	2003	
Barton, George, Buffalo, NY.	E	1903	0301	
Bassett, Dr HW, Oak Park, Ill, site.	MC	1894	9402	74
Bazett, Sidney, Hillsborough, Calif.	W	1940	4002	
Beach Cottages, Egypt, site.	E	1927	2711	
Beachy, Peter A, Oak Park, Ill.	MC	1906	0601	72
Berger, Robert, San Anselmo, Calif.	W	1950	5039	
Beth Sholom Synagogue, Elkins Park, Penn.	E	1954	5313	
Bitter Root Inn, Darby, Montana, site.	W	1909	0918	
Blair, Quinton, Cody, Wyoming.	W	1952	5203	
Blossom, George, Chicago, Ill.	MC	1892	9201	123
Bogk, Frederick C, Milwaukee, Wisc.	UGL	1916	1602	85

Boomer, Jorgine, Phoenix, Ariz.	W	1953	5302	
Booth, Sherman, House, Glencoe, Ill.	**MC**	**1915**	**1502**	**26**
Cottage.	**MC**	**1911**	**1119**	**32**
Ravine Bluffs Development, housing.	**MC**	**1915**	**1516s**	**25**
Lot 10: Perry, Charles R.	**MC**	**1915**	**1516**	**27**
Lot 15: Ellis, CJ (Kier, William F).	**MC**	**1916**	**1605**	**29**
Lot 16: Finch, Frank (Ross, William F).	**MC**	**1915**	**1516**	**30**
Lot 17: Compton, JM (Kissam, Lute F).	**MC**	**1915**	**1516**	**31**
Lot 22: Gilfillan, SJ (Root, Hollis R).	**MC**	**1915**	**1516**	**28**
Borah, Al, Barrington Hills, Ill.	**MC**	**1957**	**5518**	**47**
Boswell, William P, Indian Hill, Ohio.	E	1957	5704	
Bott, Frank, Kansas City, Mo.	W	1956	5627	
Boulter, Cedric G, Cincinnati, Ohio.	E	1954	5403	
Boynton, Edward E, Rochester, NY.	E	1908	0801	
Bradley, R Harley, Kankakee, Ill.	E	1900	0002	
Bramson Dress Shop, Oak Park, Ill, site.	**MC**	**1937**	**3706**	**74**
Brandes, Ray, Issaquah, Washington.	W	1952	5204	
Brauner, Erling, Okemos, Mich.	UGL	1948	4601	109
Brigham, Edmund F, Glencoe, Ill.	**MC**	**1915**	**1503**	**34**
Brown, Charles A, Evanston, Ill.	**MC**	**1905**	**0503**	**39**
Brown, Eric V, Kalamazoo, Mich.	UGL	1959	5003	127
Brownes Bookstore, Chicago, site.	**MC**	**1907**	**0802**	**134**
Bubilian, AH, Rochester, Minn.	UGL	1947	4709	29
Buehler, Maynard P, Orinda, Calif.	W	1948	4805	
Burhans-Ellinwod & Co, Chicago, Ill.	**MC**	**1917**	**1506**	**129**
Burleigh see O'Connor, JJ, Wilmette, Ill.	**MC**	**1916**	**1506**	**37**
Carlson, Raymond, Phoenix, Ariz.	W	1950	5004	
Carr, John O, Glenview, Ill.	**MC**	**1950**	**5014**	**48**
Carr, WS, Grand Beach, Mich.	UGL	1916	1603	133
Cass, William, New York City, Staten Island, NY.	E	1959	5518	
Chahroudi, AK, Lake Mahopac, New York, NY.	E	1951	5104	
Charnley, James, Chicago, Ill.	**MC**	**1891**	**9001**	**132**
Ocean Springs, Miss.	E	1890	9101	
Cheney, Edwin H, Oak Park, Ill.	**MC**	**1904**	**0401**	**84**
Christian, John E, West Lafayette, Ind.	E	1954	5405	
Christie, James B, Bernardsville, NJ.	E	1940	4003	

Circle Pines Resort, Cloverdale, Mich, site.	UGL	1942	4205	119
City National Bank & Hotel, Mason City, Iowa.	W	1909	0902	
Clark, W Irving, La Grange, Ill.	**MC**	**1893**	**9209**	**103**
Community Church, Kansas City, Mo.	W	1940	4004	
Como Orchard, Darby, Mont, site.	W	1910	1002	
Compton, JM, Lot 17, Ravine Bluffs, Glencoe.	**MC**	**1915**	**1516**	**31**
Cooke, Andrew, Virginia Beach, Virginia.	E	1953	5219	
Coonley, Avery, Riverside, Ill.	**MC**	**1908**	**0803**	**91**
Coonley Playhouse, Riverside, Ill.	**MC**	**1912**	**1201**	**93**
Copeland, William H, Oak Park, Ill.	**MC**	**1909**	**0904**	**66**
Crystal Heights, Washington DC, site.	E	1939	4016	
Cummings Real Estate, River Forest, Ill, site.	**MC**	**1907**	**0702**	**59**
Currier Gallery of Art, Zimmerman House,				
Manchester, NH.	E	1950	5214	
Dallas Theater Center.	W	1955	5514	
Dana, Susan Lawrence, Springfield, Ill.	E	1904	9905	
Davenport, E Arthur, River Forest, Ill.	**MC**	**1901**	**0101**	**57**
Davidson, Walter V, Buffalo, NY.	E	1908	0804	
Davis, Richard, Marion, Indiana.	E	1950	5037	
Death Valley, Calif, Johnson & Wright, sites.	W	1921	2306	
Deephaven – see Little, Francis W.	UGL	1913	1304	137
Library, Allentown, Penn.	E/UGL	1912	1304	
Metropolitan Museum, New York, NY.	E	1912	1304	
Deertrack – see Roberts, Abby.	UGL	1936	3603	97
DeRhodes, KC, South Bend, Ind.	E	1906	0602	
Dobkins, John J, Canton, Ohio	E	1954	5407	
Duncan, Don, Lisle, Ill.	**MC**	**1957**	**5518**	**99**
Edwards, James, Okemos, Mich.	UGL	1949	4904	110
Elam, SP, Austin, Minn.	UGL	1951	5105	30
Ellis, CJ, Lot 15, Ravine Bluffs, Glencoe, Ill.	**MC**	**1916**	**1605**	**29**
Emmond, Robert G, La Grange, Ill.	**MC**	**1892**	**9202**	**104**
Ennis, Charles, Los Angeles, Calif.	W	1924	2401	
Erdman Prefab houses, Upper Great Lakes				
Iber, Frank, Plover, Wisc.	UGL	1957	5518	34
Jackson, Arnold, Madison.	UGL	1957	5518	67
La Fond, St Joseph, Minn.	UGL	1960	5518	20

McBean, James, Rochester, Minn.	UGL	1957	5706	27
Mollica, Joseph, Bayside, Wisc.	UGL	1958	5518	77
Rudin, Walter, Madison.	UGL	1957	5706	61
Van Tamlen, Eugene, Madison.	UGL	1956	5518	60
Erdman Prefab houses, MetroChicago				
Borah, Al, Barrington Hills, Ill.	**MC**	**1957**	**5518**	**47**
Duncan, Don, Lisle, Ill.	**MC**	**1957**	**5518**	**99**
Erdman Prefab houses, East				
Cass, William, New York City, NY.	E	1959	5518	
Zaferiou, Socrates, Blauvelt, NY.	E	1961	5518	
Eppstein, Samuel, Galesburg, Mich.	UGL	1949	4905	121
Euchtman, Joseph, Baltimore, Maryland.	E	1940	4005	
Evans, Raymond W, Chicago, Ill.	**MC**	**1908**	**0805**	**128**
Exhibition House, New York City, NY, site.	E	1953	5314	
E-Z Polish Factory, Chicago, Ill.	**MC**	**1905**	**0504**	**117**
Fabyan, George, Geneva, Ill.	**MC**	**1907**	**0703**	**96**
Fallingwater – see Kaufmann, Edgar.	E	1936	3602	
Fasbender Medical Clinic, Hastings, Minn.	UGL	1957	5730	26
Fawcett, Randall, Los Banos, Calif.	W	1955	5418	
Feiman, Ellis A, Canton, Ohio.	E	1954	5408	
Finch, Frank B, Lot 16, Ravine Bluffs, Glencoe	**MC**	**1915**	**1516**	**30**
Fir Tree, Friedman, Pecos, NM.	W	1952	4512	
Florida Southern College: Lakeland, Fla.	E	1938	3805	
Administration Building.	E	1945	3805	
Danforth Chapel.	E	1954	3805	
Industrial Arts Building.	E	1942	3805	
Pfeiffer Chapel.	E	1938	3805	
Roux Library.	E	1941	3805	
Science Building.	E	1953	3805	
Seminar Buildings.	E	1940	3805	
Fountainhead, Hughes, Jackson, Miss.	E	1949	4908	
Foster, Stephen A, Chicago, Ill.	**MC**	**1900**	**0003**	**131**
Fox River Country Club, Geneva, Ill, site.	**MC**	**1907**	**0704**	**96**
Francis Apartments, Chicago, Ill, site.	**MC**	**1895**	**9501**	**121**
Francisco Terrace, Oak Park (formerly Chicago), site.	**MC**	**1895**	**9502**	**89**
Frederick, Louis B, Barrington Hills, Ill.	**MC**	**1954**	**5426**	**46**

Freeman, Samuel, Los Angeles, Calif.	W	1923	2402	
Freeman, Warren H, Hinsdale, Ill.	**MC**	**1903**	**0312**	**100**
Fricke, William G, Oak Park, Ill.	**MC**	**1901**	**0201**	**85**
Friedman, Allan, Bannockburn, Ill.	**MC**	**1959**	**5624**	**20**
Friedman, Arnold, Pecos, NM.	W	1945	4512	
Friedman, Sol, Pleasantville, New York, NY.	E	1949	4906	
Fuller, Grace, Glencoe, Ill, site.	**MC**	**1906**	**0603**	**34**
Fuller, Welbie, Pass Christian, Miss, site.	E	1951	5106	
Fukuhara, Arinobu, Hakone, Japan.	W	1918	1801	
Furbeck, George, Oak Park, Ill.	**MC**	**1897**	**9701**	**88**
Furbeck, Rollin, Oak Park, Ill.	**MC**	**1897**	**9801**	**86**
Gakuen School, Tokyo, Japan.	W	1921	2101	
Gale, Cottages, Whitehall, Mich.	UGL	1905	0502	102
Gale, (Mrs Thomas) Laura, Oak Park, Ill.	**MC**	**1909**	**0905**	**71**
Gale, Summer House, Whitehall, Mich.	UGL	1897	0522	101
Gale, Thomas H, Oak Park, Ill.	**MC**	**1892**	**9203**	**61**
Gale, Walter M, Oak Park, Ill.	**MC**	**1893**	**9302**	**60**
Galesburg Country Home Acres, Mich.	UGL	1948	4828	119
Gammage Memorial Auditorium, Tempe, Ariz.	W	1959	5904	
German Warehouse, Richland Center, Wisc.	UGL	1915	1504	39
Gerts, George, Duplex, Whitehall, Mich.	UGL	1902	0202	104
Gerts, Walter, Cottage, Whitehall, Mich.	UGL	1902	0205	103
Gerts, Walter, River Forest, Ill,	**MC**	**1911**	**1114**	**59**
Gillin, John A, Dallas, Texas.	W	1950	5034	
Gilfillan, SJ, Ravine Bluffs, Lot 22, Glencoe, Ill.	**MC**	**1915**	**1516**	**28**
Gilmore, Eugene A, Madison, Wisc.	UGL	1908	0806	57
Glasner, William A, Glencoe, Ill.	**MC**	**1905**	**0505**	**33**
Glenlloyd – see Bradley, R Harley.	E	1900	0002	
Glore, Herbert F, Lake Forest, Ill.	**MC**	**1951**	**5107**	**19**
Goan, Peter, La Grange, Ill.	**MC**	**1893**	**9403**	**105**
Goddard, Lewis H, Plymouth, Mich.	UGL	1953	5317	114
Goetsch-Winkler, Okemos, Mich.	UGL	1939	3907	108
Goodrich, Harry C, Oak Park, Ill.	**MC**	**1896**	**9601**	**83**
Gordon, Conrad E, Wilsonville, Oregon.	W	1957	5710	
Grady Gammage Auditorium, Tempe, Ariz.	W	1959	5904	
Grant, Douglas, Cedar Rapids, Iowa.	W	1946	4503	

Grayclff, Martin, DD, Derby, NY.	E	1927	2701	
Greek Orthodox Church, Wauwatosa, Wisc.	UGL	1956	5611	83
Greenberg, Maurice, Dousman, Wisc.	UGL	1954	5409	75
Greene, William B, Aurora, Ill.	**MC**	**1912**	**1203**	**98**
Gridley, AW, Batavia, Ill.	**MC**	**1906**	**0604**	**97**
Griggs, Chauncey L, Tacoma, Wash.	W	1946	4604	
Guggenheim Museum, New York, NY.	E	1956	4305	
Hagan, Isaac Newton, Ohiopyle, Penn.	E	1954	4510	
Hanna, Paul, Palo Alto, Calif.	W	1937	3701	
Hanney & Son, Evanston, Ill.	**MC**	**1916**	**1506**	**38**
Hardy, Thomas P, Racine, Wisc.	UGL	1905	0506	94
Harlan, Dr Allison, Chicago, Ill, site.	**MC**	**1892**	**9204**	
Harper, Ina Morris, St Joseph, Mich.	UGL	1959	5010	129
Hayashi, Aisaku, Tokyo, Japan.	W	1917	1702	
Haynes, John, Fort Wayne, Ind.	E	1951	5110	
Heath, William R, Buffalo, NY.	E	1905	0507	
Hebert, AW, Evanston, Ill.	**MC**	**1902**	**0112**	**40**
Asbury Avenue.	**MC**	**1902**		**41**
Davis Street.	**MC**	**1902**		**41**
Heller, Isadore, Chicago, Ill.	**MC**	**1896**	**9606**	**124**
Henderson, FB, Elmhurst, Ill.	**MC**	**1901**	**0104**	**102**
Heurtley, Arthur, Oak Park, Ill.	**MC**	**1902**	**0204**	**70**
Cottage, Marquette Island, Mich.	UGL	1902	0214	98
Hickox, Warren, Kankakee, Ill.	E	1900	0004	
Hills, Edward R, Oak Park, Ill.	**MC**	**1906**	**0102**	**69**
Hillside Home School, Taliesin, Spring Green, Wisc.	UGL	1902	0216	46
Hoffman, Max, Rye, New York, NY.	E	1955	5535	
Hoffman Showroom, New York, NY.	E	1956	5622	
Hollyhock House – see Barnsdall, Aline.	W	1917	1705	
Home & Studio, Oak Park, Ill – Wright, Frank Lloyd.	**MC**	**1889**	**8901**	**63**
Honeycomb House – see Hanna, Paul.	W	1937	3701	
Horner, LK, Chicago, Ill, site.	**MC**	**1908**	**0807**	**113**
Horse Show Association Fountain, Oak Park, Ill.	**MC**	**1908**	**0305**	**77**
Horseshoe Inn, Estes Park, Colo, site.	W	1908	0814	
Hoyt, PD, Geneva, Ill.	**MC**	**1906**	**0605**	**95**
Hughes, J Willis, Jackson, Miss.	E	1949	4908	

Humphries Theater, Dallas, Texas.	W	1955	5514	
Hunt, Stephen MB, La Grange, Ill.	**MC**	**1907**	**0705**	**106**
Hunt, Stephen MB, Oshkosh, Wisc.	UGL	1917	1703	35
Husser, Joseph J, Chicago, Ill, site.	**MC**	**1899**	**9901**	**114**
Hyde, H Howard, Chicago, Ill.	**MC**	**1917**	**1506**	**130**
Iber, Frank, Plover, Wisc.	UGL	1957	5518	34
Imperial Hotel, Tokyo, Japan, original site.	W	1915	1509	
Imperial Hotel Reconstruction, Nagoya, Japan.	W	1976	1509	
Ingalls, J Kibben, River Forest, Ill.	**MC**	**1909**	**0906**	**56**

The entry to the now demolished Joseph W Husser House, Chicago, Ill, c 1899

Irving, Edward P, Decatur, Ill.	E	1910	1003	
Jackson, Arnold, Beaver Dam, formerly Madison, Wisc.	UGL	1957	5518	67
Jacobs, Herbert, I, Madison, Wisc.	UGL	1936	3702	56
Jacobs, Herbert, II, Middleton, Wisc.	UGL	1948	4812	54
Jiyu Gakuen School, Japan.	W	1921	2101	
Johnson, AP, Delavan, Wisc.	UGL	1905	0508	74
Johnson, Herbert F, Wingspread, Wind Point, Wisc.	UGL	1937	3703	88
Johnson, Oscar, see Hanney & Son, Evanston, Ill.	**MC**	**1917**	**1506**	**38**
Johnson Wax Company, Racine, Wisc.	UGL	1936	3601	91
Jones, Fred B, Delavan, Wisc.	UGL	1900	0103	72
Gatehouse	UGL	1900	0103	71
Jones, Richard Lloyd, Tulsa, Okla.	W	1929	2902	
Juvenile Cultural Center, Wichita, Kansas.	W	1957	5743	
Kalil, Toufik, Manchester, NH.	E	1955	5506	
Kansas City Community Christian Church.	W	1040	4004	
Kaufmann, Edgar, Fallingwater, Mill Run, Penn.	E	1936	3602	
Kaufmann Office, now London, England.	E	1937	3704	
Keland, Willard H, Racine, Wisc.	UGL	1954	5417	90
Keys, Thomas E, Rochester, Minn.	UGL	1950	5012	28
Kier, William F, Ravine Bluffs (Lot 15), Glencoe, Ill.	**MC**	**1915**	**1516**	**28**
Kinney, Patrick, Lancaster, Wisc.	UGL	1951	5038	38
Kinney, Sterling, Amarillo, Texas.	W	1957	5717	
Kissam, Daniel E, Ravine Bluffs (Lot 17), Glencoe, Ill.	**MC**	**1915**	**1516**	**31**
Kraus, Russel, Kirkwood, Mo.	W	1951	5123	
Kundert Medical Clinic, San Luis Obisbo, Calif.	W	1956	5614	
LaFond, Dr Edward, St Joseph, Minn.	UGL	1960	5518	20
Lake Delavan Yacht Club, Delavan, Wisc, site.	UGL	1902	0217	68
Lake Geneva Hotel, Lake Geneva, Wisc, site.	UGL	1912	1202	68
Lake Tahoe Summer Colony, site.	W	1922	2205	
Lamberson, Jack, Oskaloosa, Iowa.	W	1947	4712	
La Miniatura, Millard, Alice, Pasadena, Calif.	W	1923	2302	
Lamp, Robert M, Madison, Wisc.	UGL	1903	0402	59
Lamp, Robert M, Rockyroost, Madison, Wisc, site.	UGL	1893	9301	58
Larkin Building, Buffalo, NY, site.	E	1903	0403	
Laurent, Kenneth, Rockford, Ill.	UGL	1949	4814	135
Laurent, Kenneth, Rockford, Ill.	**MC**	**1949**	**4814**	**43**

Lawrence Memorial Library, Springfield, Ill.	E	1905	0509
Levin, Robert, Kalamazoo, Mich.	UGL	1949	4911	125
Lewis, George, Talahassee, Fla.	E	1952	5207
Lewis, Lloyd, Libertyville, Ill.	**MC**	**1940**	**4008**	**17**
Lincoln Center (Abraham), Chicago, Ill.	**MC**	**1903**	**0010**	**120**
Lindholm, RW, Cloquet, Minn.	UGL	1952	5208	19
Lindholm, Service Station, Cloquet, Minn.	UGL	1957	5739	18
Little, Francis W, Peoria, Ill.	E	1902	0009
Living-room, Metropolitan Museum of Art, New York City, NY.	E	1982	1304
Original site, Deephaven, Minn.	UGL	1913	1304	137
Library, Allentown Museum of Art, Penn.	E	1988	1304
Little Dipper, Barnsdall, Los Angeles, Calif.	W	1921	2301
Lockridge Medical Clinic, Whitefish, Montana.	W	1958	5813
Lovness, Donald, House, Stillwater, Minn.	UGL	1955	5507	24
Lovness, Donald, Cottage, Stillwater, Minn.	UGL	1955	5824	25
Lykes, Norman, Phoenix, Arizona.	W	1966	5908
MacHarg, William, Chicago, Ill, site.	**MC**	**1891**	**9002**	**114s**
Manson, Charles L, Wausau, Wisc.	UGL	1940	4009	32
Marcus, Stanley, Dallas, Texas, site.	W	1935	3501
Marden, Louis, McLean, Va.	E	1952	5220
Marin County Civic Center, San Rafel, Calif.	W	1957	5746
Martin, Darwin D, Buffalo, NY.	E	1904	0405
Martin, DD, Gardener's Cottage, Buffalo, NY.	E	1905	0530
Martin, DD, Graycliff, Derby, New York, NY.	E	1927	2701
Martin, William E, Oak Park, Ill.	**MC**	**1902**	**0304**	**82**
Mathews, Arthur C, Atherton, Calif.	W	1950	5013
May, Meyer, Grand Rapids, Mich.	UGL	1908	0817	105
McArthur, Warren, Chicago, Ill.	**MC**	**1892**	**9205**	**122**
McBean, James B, Rochester, Minn.	UGL	1957	5706	27
McCartney, Ward, Kalamazoo, Mich.	UGL	1949	4912	128
McCormick, Harold, Lake Forest, Ill, site.	**MC**	**1907**	**0713**	**19**
Meier, Delbert W, Monona, Iowa.	W	1917	1506
Meiji Mura Museum, Imperial Hotel, Japan.	W	1915	1509
Mendota Boathouse, Madison, Wisc.	UGL	1893	9304	58
Metropolitan Museum of Art, Little House,			

living room, New York City, NY.	E	1912	1304	
Meyer, Curtis, Galesburg, Mich.	UGL	1950	5015	122
Meyers Medical Clinic, Dayton, Ohio.	E	1956	5613	
Midway Gardens, Chicago, III, site.	**MC**	**1914**	**1401**	**126**
Millard, Alice, Pasadena, Calif.	W	1923	2302	
Millard, George Madison, Highland Park, III.	**MC**	**1906**	**0606**	**22**
Miller, Alvin, Charles City, Iowa.	W	1946	5016	
Miller, Arthur and Marilyn Monroe, site.	E	1957	5719	
Moe, Ingwald, Gary, Ind.	**MC**	**1908**	**0531**	**110**
Mollica, Joseph, Bayside, Wisc.	UGL	1958	5518	77
Monona Terrace, Madison, site.	UGL	1938	3909	58
Monroe, Marilyn and Arthur Miller, site	E	1957	5719	
Moore, Nathan G, Oak Park, III.	**MC**	**1895**	**9503**	**68**
Mori Art Shop, Chicago, III, site.	**MC**	**1914**	**1402**	**134**
Morris Gift Shop, San Francisco, Calif.	W	1948	4824	
Mossberg, Herman T, South Bend, Ind.	E	1949	4914	
Muirhead, Robert, Plato Center, III.	**MC**	**1950**	**5019**	**45**
Municipal Boathouse, Madison, Wisc, site.	UGL	1893	9308	58
Munkwitz Duplex, Milwaukee, Wisc, site.	UGL	1916	1606	79

The entry to the now demolished Midway Gardens, Chicago, III, c 1914

Nakoma Country Club, Madison, Wisc, site.	UGL	1924	2403	52
Neils, Henry J, Minneapolis, Minn.	UGL	1950	5020	22
Nicholas, Frederick D, Flossmoor, Ill.	**MC**	**1906**	**0607**	**108**
Northome, Little House, site.	UGL	1912	1304	137
Little House, library, Allentown, Penn.	E	1912	1304	
Little House, living room, New York City, NY.	E	1912	1304	
Oboler, Gatehouse, Malibu, Calif.	W	1941	4112	
Ocatillo Camp, Chandler, Ariz, site.	W	1928	2702	
O'Connor, JJ, Wilmette, Ill.	**MC**	**1917**	**1506**	**37**
Odawara Hotel, Japan, site.	W	1917	1706	
Olfelt, Paul, St Louis Park, Minn.	UGL	1958	5820	21
Palmer, William, Ann Arbor, Mich.	UGL	1950	5021	118
Pappas, Theodore A St Louis, Mo.	W	1955	5516	
Park Ridge Country Club, Park Ridge, Ill, site.	**MC**	**1912**	**1204**	**48**
Parker, Robert P, Oak Park, Ill.	**MC**	**1892**	**9206**	**62**
Parkwyn Village, Kalamazoo, Mich.	UGL	1948	4806	124
Pauson, Rose, Phoenix, Ariz, site.	W	1940	4011	
Pearce, Wilbur, Bradbury, Calif.	W	1951	5114	
Pebbles & Balch shop, Oak Park, Ill, site.	**MC**	**1907**	**0708**	**75**

Nathan Moore House after the fire in 1922, Oak Park, Ill, c 1895

Penfield, Louis, Willoughby Hills, Ohio.	E	1953	5303	
Perry, Charles R, Ravine Bluffs, Glencoe, Ill.	**MC**	**1915**	**1516**	**27**
Peterson, Seth, Lake Delton, Wisc.	UGL	1958	5821	37
Pettit Memorial Chapel, Belvidere, Ill.	UGL	1906	0619	136
Pettit Memorial Chapel, Belvidere, Ill.	**MC**	**1906**	**0619**	**44**
Pew, John C, Shorewood Hills, Wisc.	UGL	1940	4012	64
Pieper, Arthur, Paradise Valley, Phoenix, Ariz.	W	1952	5218	
Pilgrim Congregational Church, Redding, Calif.	W	1959	5318	
Pitkin, EH, Desbarats, Ontario, Canada.	UGL	1900	0005	96
Plaza Hotel Apartment, FLW, New York City, NY.	E	1955	5532	
Pope-Leighy House, Woodlawn, Virginia.	E	1940	4013	
Porter, Andrew T, Spring Green, Wisc.	UGL	1907	0709	48
Post Office, Marin County, Calif.	W	1957	5746	
Post, Frederick B see Al Borah, Barrington Hills, Ill.	**MC**	**1957**	**5518**	**47**
Pratt, Eric, Galesburg, Mich.	UGL	1948	4827	120
Price, Harold Jr, Bartlesville, Okla.	W	1954	5421	
Price, Harold, Sr, Paradise Valley, Phoenix, Ariz.	W	1954	5421	
Price Tower, Bartelsville, Okla.	W	1952	5215	
Ras El Bar, Egypt, site.	E	1927	7211	
Ravine Bluffs Development, Glencoe, Ill.	**MC**	**1915**	**1516**	**25**
Ravine Bluffs Housing				
Lot 10: Perry, Charles R.	**MC**	**1915**	**1516**	**27**
Lot 15: Ellis, CJ.	**MC**	**1915**	**1516**	**29**
Lot 16: Finch, Frank B.	**MC**	**1915**	**1516**	**30**
Lot 17: Compton, JM.	**MC**	**1915**	**1516**	**31**
Lot 22: Gilfillan, SJ.	**MC**	**1915**	**1516**	**28**
Rayward, John L, New Canaan, Conn.	E	1955	5523	
Rebhuhn, Ben, Great Neck Estates, NY.	E	1937	3801	
Reisley, Roland, Pleasantville, NY.	E	1951	5115	
Richards Co of Milwaukee see American Systems Bungalow,				
Richardson, Stuart, Glen Ridge, NJ.	E	1941	4104	
River Forest Golf Club, Ill, site.	**MC**	**1898**	**9802**	**59**
River Forest Tennis Club, Ill.	**MC**	**1906**	**0510**	**58**
Riverview Terrace Restaurant, Spring Green, Wisc.	UGL	1956	5619	45
Roberts, Abby Beecher, Marquette, Mich.	UGL	1936	3603	97
Roberts, Charles E, Oak Park, Ill.	**MC**	**1896**	**9603**	**87**

Roberts, Isabel, River Forest, Ill.	**MC**	**1908**	**0808**	**55**
Robie, Frederick C, Chicago, Ill.	**MC**	**1909**	**0908**	**125**
Rockyroost, Lamp, Robert M, Madison, site.	UGL	1893	9301	58
Roloson, Robert W, Row Houses, Chicago, Ill.	**MC**	**1894**	**9404**	**119**
Romeo and Juliet Windmill, Spring Green, Wisc.	UGL	1896	9607	49
Rookery Building Lobby, Chicago, Ill.	**MC**	**1905**	**0511**	**135**
Root, Hollis R, Ravine Bluffs (Lot 22), Glencoe, Ill.	**MC**	**1915**	**1516**	**28**
Rosenbaum, Florence, Ala.	E	1939	3903	
Ross, Charles S, Delavan, Wisc.	UGL	1902	0206	70
Ross, William W, Ravine Bluffs (Lot 16), Glencoe, Ill.	**MC**	**1915**	**1516**	**30**
Roux Library, Florida Southern College, Lakeland, Fla.	E	1941	3805	
Rubin, Nathan, Canton, Ohio.	E	1951	5116	
Rudin, Walter, Madison, Wisc.	UGL	1957	5706	61
San Marcos in the Desert, site.	W	1928	2704	
St Marks in the Bowrie, New York City, NY, site.	E	1929	2905	
Sander, Frank S, Stamford, Conn.	E	1953	5304	
Schaberg, Donald, Okemos, Mich.	UGL	1950	5022	111
Schultz, Carl, St Joseph, Mich.	UGL	1957	5745	130
Schwartz, Bernard, Two Rivers, Wisc.	UGL	1939	3904	36
Scoville Park Fountain, Oak Park, Ill.	**MC**	**1909**	**0305**	**77**
Scully, Vincent, site.	E	1948	4816	
Serlin, Edward, Pleasantville, NY.	E	1949	4917	
Shavin, Seamour, Chattanooga, Tenn.	E	1950	5023	
Smith Bank, Dwight, Ill.	E	1905	0512	
Smith, George W, Oak Park, Ill.	**MC**	**1896**	**9803**	**78**
Smith, Melvin Maxwell, Bloomfield Hills, Mich.	UGL	1949	4818	116
Smith, Richard, Jefferson, Wisc.	UGL	1959	5026	65
Snowflake, Wall, Carlton D, Plymouth, Mich.	UGL	1941	4114	113
Sondern, Clarence, Kansas City, Mo.	W	1940	4014	
Spencer, Dudley, Wilmington, Delaware.	E	1956	5605	
Spencer, George W, Delavan, Wisc.	UGL	1902	0207	69
Staley, Karl A, North Madison, Ohio.	E	1951	5119	
Steffens, Oscar, Chicago, Ill, site.	**MC**	**1909**	**0909**	**113**
Steinway Hall, Chicago, Ill, site.	MC	-	-	134
Stevens, C Leigh, Auldbrass Plantation, Yemassee, SC.	E	1940	4015	
Stewart, George C, Monteceto, Calif.	W	1909	0907	

Stockman, GC, Mason City, Iowa.	W	1908	0809
Stohr Arcade, Chicago, Ill, site.	**MC**	**1909**	**0910** **114**
Storer, John, Los Angeles, Hollywood, Calif.	W	1923	2304
Stromquist, Donald, Bountiful, Utah.	W	1958	5626
Sturges, Brentwood Heights, Calif.	W	1939	3905
Sugarloaf Mountain, Strong, Maryland, site.	E	1924	2505
Sullivan, Louis (Albert), Chicago, Ill, site.	**MC**	**1892**	**9207** **121**
Sullivan, Louis, Ocean Springs, Miss.	E	1890	9003
Sunday, Robert H, Marshalltown, Iowa.	W	1955	5522
Suntop Homes, Ardmore, Penn.	E	1939	3906
Sutton, Harvey P, McCook, Nebr.	W	1907	0710
Sweeton, JA, Cherry Hill, NJ.	E	1959	5027
Taliesin, Spring Green, Wisc.	UGL	1911	1104 42
Taliesin West, Scottsdale, Ariz.	W	1938	3803
Tan-y-deri, Porter, Andrew D, Spring Green, Wisc.	UGL	1907	0709 48
Teater, Archie B, Bliss, Idaho.	W	1952	5211
Thaxton, William L, Bunker Hill, Texas.	W	1954	5414
Thomas, Frank W, Oak Park, Ill.	**MC**	**1901**	**0106** **73**
Thurber Art Gallery, Chicago, Ill, site.	**MC**	**1909**	**0911** **134**

The now demolished Oscar Steffens House, Chicago, Ill, c 1909

Tirranna, Rayward, John, New Canaan, Conn.	E	1955	5523
Tomek, Ferdinand F, Riverside, Ill.	**MC**	**1907**	**0711 90**
Tonkens, Gerald B, Amberly Village, Ohio.	E	1955	5510
Tracy, William B, Normandy Park, Wash.	W	1955	5512
Trier, Paul J, Johnston, Des Moines, Iowa.	W	1957	5724
Turkel, H, Detroit, Mich.	UGL	1955	5513 117
Unitarian Meeting House, Shorewood Hills, Wisc.	UGL	1947	5031 62
Unity Chapel, Spring Green, Wisc.	UGL	1886	8601 50
Unity Temple, Oak Park, Ill.	**MC**	**1906**	**0611 75**
Usonian Exhibition House, New York, NY.	E	1953	5314
Usonia Homes, Pleasantville, NY.	E	1947	4720
Vanderkloot, William J, Lake Bluff, Ill.	**MC**	**1916**	**1506 18**
Van Tamlen, Eugene, Madison, Wisc.	UGL	1956	5518 60
Vosburgh, Ernest, Grand Beach, Mich.	UGL	1916	1607 132
Walker, Clinton, Carmel, Calif.	W	1951	5122
Wall, Carlton D, Plymouth, Mich.	UGL	1941	4114 113
Waller Apartments, Chicago, Ill.	**MC**	**1895**	**9504 118**
Waller Bathing Pavilion, Charlevoix, Mich, site.	UGL	1909	0916 100
Waller, Edward C, River Forest, Ill, site.	**MC**	**1899**	**9902 49**
Wallis, Henry, Delavan, Wisc.	UGL	1900	0114 73
Walser, JJ, Chicago, Ill.	**MC**	**1903**	**0306 116**
Walter, Lowel, Quasqueton, Iowa.	W	1945	4505
Walton, Robert G, Modesto, Calif.	W	1957	5623
Weisblatt, David I, Galesburg, Mich.	UGL	1948	4918 123
Weltzheimer, Charles T, Oberlin, Ohio.	E	1948	4819
Western Pennsylvania Conservancy, Fallingwater.	E	1935	3602
Westhope, Jones, Richard Lloyd, Tulsa, Okla.	W	1929	2902
Westcott, Burton J, Springfield, Ohio.	E	1907	0712
Wiley, Malcom E, Minneapolis, Minn.	UGL	1933	3401 23
Williams, Chauncey L, River Forest, Ill.	**MC**	**1895**	**9505 54**
Willits, Ward W, Highland Park, Ill.	**MC**	**1901**	**0208 23**
Wilson, Abraham, Millstone, NJ.	E	1954	5402
Winn, Robert D, Kalamazoo, Mich.	UGL	1948	4815 126
Winslow, William Herman, River Forest, Ill.	MC	1894	9305 52
Women's Building, Spring Green, Wisc, site.	UGL	1914	1413 40
Wooley, Francis J, Oak Park, Ill.	**MC**	**1893**	**9405 67**

World's Columbian Exhibition of 1893, Chicago	**MC**	-	-	**126**
Wright, Anna L, Oak Park, Ill.	**MC**	-	-	**65**
Wright, David, Phoenix, Ariz.	E	1950	5030	
Wright, Duey, Wausau, Wisc.	UGL	1957	5727	33
Wright, Frank Lloyd,				
Apartment, Plaza, NY, site.	E	1954	5532	
House and Studio, Oak Park, Ill.	**MC**	**1889**	**8901**	**63**
Studio, Chicago, Ill, site.	**MC**	**1911**	**1113**	**133**
Studio, Los Angeles, Calif, site.	W	1922	2201	
Wright, Robert Llewellyn, Bethesda, Maryland	E	1953	5312	
Wynant, Wilber, Gary, Ind.	**MC**	**1915**	**1506**	**109**
Wyoming Valley Grammar School, Spring Green, Wisc.	UGL	1957	5741	51
Yahara Boat Club, Madison, Wisc, site.	UGL	1905	0211	58
Yamamura, Tazaemon, Ashiya, Osaka, Japan.	W	1918	1803	
Young, Harrison P, Oak Park, Ill.	**MC**	**1895**	**9507**	**79**
Zaferiou, Socrates, Blauvelt, NY	E	1961	5518	
Zeigler, Jessie R, Frankfort, Kent.	E	1910	1007	
Zimmerman, Isadore, Manchester, NH.	E	1952	5214	

Living-room interior of the Frank Lloyd Wright Home, Oak Park, Ill, c 1890